GRETCHEN M. FOSTER

Pope Versus Dryden: A Controversy in Letters to *The Gentleman's Magazine*

EDITIONS

ELS Editions
Department of English
University of Victoria
Victoria, BC
Canada V8W 3W1
www.elseditions.com

Founding Editor: Samuel L. Macey

General Editor: Luke Carson

Printed by CreateSpace

English literary studies monograph series
ISSN 0829-7681 ; 44
ISBN-10 0-920604-41-2
ISBN-13 978-0-920604-41-0

"That the dispute about Dryden and Pope was not a fortnight ago."

Wager between John Oldershaw and Hugh Wade, Fellows of Emmanuel College, for one bottle of wine.

Emmanuel College Wager Book, Cambridge University
January 10, 1792

To Arthur Sherbo

CONTENTS

ACKNOWLEDGEMENTS

I wish to acknowledge the guidance and moral support given me by Robert W. Uphaus, Professor of English, Michigan State University, and my husband, Richard B. Foster, Jr. For her help and patience in preparing the text of the letters, I wish to thank Polly McGann.

INTRODUCTION

The Nobel laureate in physics, Werner Heisenberg, has written that there are two kinds of scientists — the great theorists and those who do the practical work of making the theories work. To this effect he recalls what Schiller said about Kant: "When kings go a-building, wagoners have more work."[1] We might say the same thing about literary criticism. An Aristotle or a Coleridge lays claim to new theoretical territory, but without the wagoners who construct the interpretations, auxiliary theories, and close readings, or who describe and analyze historical and social contexts, these territories would remain remote and barren.

When, in 1789, Anna Seward and Joseph Weston entered into a debate about the merits of Alexander Pope and John Dryden, they became wagoners in the province of educated literary taste. Their extended paper war captured the reading public's notice. Literary amateurs, Cambridge dons, the renowned and the unknown, the young and the old followed, joined, and finally wearied of the flood of words their two-year conflict called forth. Tedious and trivial as it may seem to the twentieth-century reader, the Seward-Weston controversy touches on significant issues in eighteenth-century poetic theory and contributes substantially to our understanding of polite literary taste just before the Romantic revolution.

BACKGROUND OF THE CONTROVERSY

In the closing decades of the eighteenth century, Joseph Weston, an obscure organist in the small town of Solihull just southeast of Birmingham, translated into English a Latin poem, *Philotoxi Ardenae* (*The Woodmen of Arden*, 1788), by Birmingham attorney and amateur poet John Morfitt. Weston rendered Morfitt's poem first in blank verse, then in heroic couplets "in the manner of Dryden."[2] He prefaced the translation with "An Essay on the Superiority of Dryden's Versification over that of *Pope* and of the *Moderns*." Deploring the pernicious effect Pope's style had had on English poetry, he called on his readers to join him in restoring "to Drydenical Purity that Pierian Spring which Pope *corrupted*, and which his more daring *Imitators* have Poisoned!" (xxiv).

Anna Seward, a poetess and lady of letters who lived with her father in Lichfield, Samuel Johnson's birthplace, had met Weston during the winter of 1788 and found him to be a bit odd in appearance and mannerisms but also "a mine" of "wit, intelligence, and poetic genius," with "taste and real accuracy in criticism" which "enable him to cut the rich ore they produce brilliant."[3] Word that Joseph Weston had translated Morfitt's poem reached Anna Seward later that year, and in December she wrote to him, "I long to see your two translations of the Latin poem on the Woodmen of Arden" (2:206). But, a month later (January, 1789), after she had seen the poem and preface, she wrote to Weston voicing her dismay at his "strong prejudices... against the sweet Swan of Twickenham." She begged him to soften "the warmth of your censure upon Pope, since there is such an inevitably large majority of opinions against yours in both instances" (2:209-10). Three months later, *The Gentleman's Magazine* published the first installment of what it called her "Strictures on the Preface to the Woodmen of Arden." Her comments ran to more than 2,700 words; the controversy which they began lasted two years and drew letters from seventeen correspondents in addition to herself and Joseph Weston. During 1789 and 1790, each issue of the *GM* carried something about the controversy. In all, the debate ran to some 30,000 words of reasoning and opinion, quotation and counter quotation, and heated attack, rebuttal, and re-rebuttal.

The controversy introduces us to one sector of polite literary taste which existed only a few years before Wordsworth published his prefaces to the *Lyrical Ballads* in 1798 and 1800. The correspondents' discussion of such topics as poetic diction, sublimity, Pope's effect on poetry, and the state of poetry in the 1780s reveals no general sense that poetry is exhausted or that a major revolution is in the making. At the same time, it does show that the literati were thinking about the need for changes in poetry.

Although Wordsworth's prefaces provide a convenient end-of-the-century date for the revolution in poetry that the Romantics brought about, interest in the more private and emotive poetry of sensibility had been growing for at least fifty years. Anna Seward's list of eminent poets (Letter 1a) of her generation contains the names of many who were writing such poetry: Gray, Thomson, Collins, Akenside, Cowper, Burns, and Chatterton.

The debate between Anna Seward and Joseph Weston raises the essential questions asked by readers in every generation and answered in as many ways as there are literary periods and interpreters: What is poetry, and who is the true poet? Both Dryden and Pope were still considered by many critics and readers to be among England's greatest poets. Pope's reputation, especially, continued to grow after his death and remained strong with many critics and readers through the end of the century despite increasing support for the more private poetry of sensibility. In *Pope and His Critics*, W. L. MacDonald notes that editions of Pope's writings "swelled to [their] most impressive *fortissimo*" between 1751 and 1769.[4] The *Cambridge Bibliography of English Literature* lists "Seventeen editions or issues of the poet's *Works*, besides separate pieces, making in all upwards of 130 volumes" for this period, and the "list is not necessarily complete." MacDonald observes that, despite Joseph Warton's two-volume *Essay on the Genius and Writings of Pope* with its relegation of Pope to the second rank of poets, "within four years of the turn of the century, critical delirium at the height of frenzy shrieked the praises of Pope" (314).

In *The Reputation and Writings of Alexander Pope*, James Reeves disagrees with MacDonald's estimate of Pope's supremacy. He writes: "The notion that Pope was supreme... throughout the latter half of the eighteenth century, and was only dethroned with the triumph of Romanticism has so often been repeated that it is still regarded as a truism,"[5] and one which ignores Warton's critical insights at mid-century and glosses over the extent to which Samuel Johnson had reservations about Pope. Reeves goes on to say, however, that "justice has never, so far as I know, been done to Warton," and that, although Johnson is not Pope's "unequivocal, rapturous admirer," he "is usually taken to be" just that (6, 12).

William MacClintock's *Joseph Warton's Essay on Pope: A History of the Five Editions* (1933), which Reeves apparently did not know, supports Reeves's contention that Pope's reputation was not supreme during the last half of the eighteenth century. MacClintock writes, "When the *Essay* appeared in 1756, it made a decided impression — indeed, it almost created a sensation. It challenged the supremacy of Pope, whose reputation was still high. We shall see elsewhere that it was widely read and that the second volume was eagerly awaited."[6] MacClintock estimates "cautiously" that "between four and five thousand copies of the *Essay* must have been printed during Warton's lifetime" (16), that is, before 1800 when Warton died. This is a large edition by 18th-century standards.

Anna Seward's and Joseph Weston's debate mirrors this split in the assessment of Pope's reputation. It also indicates where the majority lay among those who read the *GM*. Miss Seward assumes she has opinion on her side, and Joseph Weston agrees. He anticipates that his objections to

11

Pope's supremacy are "unfavourable to *most* of my Contemporaries."[7]

In the course of this debate, Miss Seward, Weston, and all those who join in touch on many of the major critical topics that eighteenth-century comparisons of Pope and Dryden usually brought up. To appreciate the context of their arguments we must briefly examine these earlier comparisons.

PREVIOUS COMPARISONS OF POPE AND DRYDEN

Comparing Pope and Dryden was a frequent critical activity during the eighteenth century. The two poets wrote in the same verse form and many of the same genres. As Pope said to Joseph Spence, "I learned versification wholly from Dryden's works."[8] He often borrowed or echoed lines, phrases, and images from Dryden, as the Twickenham edition attests. Pope's poetry called out for comparison with Dryden's, and the critics were quick to oblige.

Dennis through Shiels (1711-1753)

The earliest comparison by a major critic was John Dennis's. A fine critic in many ways, and one who shared many of Pope's views about poetry, Dennis combined his legitimate insights into Pope's work with a violent personal antipathy.[9] He had believed himself attacked as the tyrannical and easily inflamed critic Appius in *An Essay on Criticism* (1711). Accordingly, he opened fire, calling it "a most notorious Instance of this depravity of Genius and Tast[e]" which has invaded English culture.[10] Dennis admired Dryden as much as he despised Pope. He praised him warmly for "the Power, and Variety, and Fulness of his Harmony; for the Purity, the Perspicuity, the Energy of his Expression" and the "Solemnity and Majesty of his Style."[11] He judged Pope to be "the very reverse of all this," without either "power or variety of harmony." He damned Pope's "smooth verse" as a "continuall bagpipe drone." Whereas "Mr. Dryden's expressions are always worthy of his thoughts" Pope "never speaks nor thinks at all; or, which is all one, his language is frequently as barbarous, as his thoughts are false." As for Dryden's faults, Dennis declared, "Wherever Genius runs thro' a Work, I forgive its Faults, and where that is wanting no Beauties can touch me."

Dennis's comparison, extreme though it was, identified some of the features that future critics would develop. Dryden was vigorous, original and majestic; Pope was smooth, and unoriginal. Dennis made one

12

charge that only Joseph Weston was to take up later.[12] Pope's praise of Dryden was false. Had Dryden been alive, Pope would have vented his "Pride and Malice" on him. Further, Pope allowed his admirers to heighten his own reputation at the expense of Dryden's.

Just as Pope's enemies consistently ranked him far below Dryden, so his sympathizers, especially his early biographers, while recognizing his debt to Dryden, typically ranked him above the older poet. William Ayre reflected such opinions when he wrote that Pope "exceeded [Dryden] as well in the Copiousness of his Subject, as in the Sharpness of his Pen." Ayre was one of the earliest writers to contrast Dryden's habits of hasty composition and lack of revision with Pope's constant and meticulous polishing of his verse which led him to "keep a Piece Years by him, and have the Approbation of all whose Judgments he depended upon, before he would let the publick Eye pass over it.[13]

A much more extended and significant comparison by Robert Shiels (one of Samuel Johnson's amanuenses for the *Dictionary*) appeared at mid-century. Like critics before and after him, Shiels found that, although Dryden had done much to smooth and polish English verse, Pope had done still more. Dryden's lines "with all their smoothness were often rambling." Pope's verse was "compleatly musical" as well as "minutely correct." Shiels seemed to view this as a mixed blessing and wondered "whether the ear is not apt to be soon cloy'd with this uniformity of elegance, this sameness of harmony."[14] Thirty-five years later, Joseph Weston and his adherents did more than wonder about this. John Morfitt spoke for the anti-Pope side when he asserted that Pope's "*cuckoo* notes disgust my ear; the interminable level tires; and I pant for hill and dale" (Letter 9).

As Joseph Warton and Edward Young were to do a few years later, Shiels noted that "the grand characteristic of a poet is his invention, the surest distinction of a great genius." But, while Warton and Young would charge Pope with lack of imaginative invention, Shiels found that, for originality, Pope's *Rape of the Lock* was "without a rival in our language, for Dryden has written nothing of the kind" (5:249). In satire, Pope excelled Dryden, whereas Dryden triumphed in the lyric. For Shiels, superiority in lyric poetry categorically raised Dryden over Pope because "the Lyric is a more excellent kind of writing than the Satiric; and consequently he who excells in the most excellent species, must undoubtedly be esteemed the greatest poet" (5:249).

Shiels's final comparison of the two highlighted the art versus nature and judgment versus wit paradigms of which eighteenth-century critics were so fond and which Samuel Johnson[15] would pursue some thirty years later. Shiels found Pope's highly articulated and refined art inferior to Dryden's robust and varied poetry with its "poignant discoveries of wit" and its "general knowledge of the humours and characters of men," he extended to Dryden and Pope the popular comparison in which Homer was superior to Virgil and Shakespeare to Ben Jonson because the former had more nature and wit while the latter had more art and judgment. Thus, "We admire Dryden as the greater genius, and Pope as the most pleasing versifier" (5:252).

Three years after Shiels's comparison of Pope and Dryden appeared, Joseph Warton published the first volume of his two-volume *Essay on the Genius and Writings of Pope*. He dedicated it to Edward Young, who shared many of his views about poetry and who, a few years later, published his own *Conjectures on Original Composition*. Warton distinguished between the moral and didactic poetry of Pope and Dryden and what he called "true poetry," which arose from a "warm and glowing imagination."[16] Warton published the second volume of his *Essay* in 1782, a few years before the Seward-Weston controversy, so his comparison of Pope and Dryden would have been fresh in the controversialists' minds.

Joseph Warton's Essay *(1756-1782)*

Warton's comparison of the two poets combined traditional views with new ideas about the importance of imagination, sublimity, and emotion or, as he put it, pathos. Warton found that comparing Pope with Dryden was particularly appropriate because Dryden "was the constant pattern of Pope" (2:12). The terms in which he characterized them followed the familiar eighteenth-century models of nature versus art, wit versus judgment. Accordingly, he found Pope's poetry showed great judgment and art. His language was elegant and appropriately elevated, although he could use simple language to good effect at times. His versification could become monotonous, as in his translation of the *Iliad*, in which his scrupulous avoidance of the Alexandrine caused it to fall "into an unpleasing and tiresome monotony" (1:143). Dryden, by contrast, was sprightly, witty, flexible, exuberant, and natural. Although Pope used "common and familiar words" from time to time, Dryden used them more freely, giving "a secret charm, and a natural air to his verses, well knowing of what consequence it was sometimes to soften and subdue his tints, and not to paint and adorn every object he touched with perpetual pomp, and unremitted splendor" (2:170-71).

In his final assessment of Pope as compared with Dryden, Warton commented on Pope's "correctness" (2:404). Earlier, he had noted that the "principal merit of the Pastorals of Pope consists, in their correct and musical versification" and that in this form of poetry he had "lengthened the abruptness of Waller, and at the same time contracted the exuberance of Dryden" (1:10). Perhaps there is a note of regret here for that contracted and corrected exuberance. Dryden, of course, was open to no such criticism. Whether by choice or necessity, he had avoided the stultifying effects of too much refining and reworking. This does not mean that Warton believed Dryden was by nature careless about the use of language. He noted that Dryden was the Earl of Roscommon's "principal assistance" in planning "a society for the refining and fixing the standard of our language" (1:192).

Warton carefully compared the two poets in every possible genre, sometimes finding Pope superior, sometimes Dryden and sometimes just noting that their achievements differed, without one necessarily being superior to the other. Overall, he found that Pope excelled Dryden in craftsmanship, artistry, and consistent moral reasoning, but in one poem at least, *Alexander's Feast, or the Power of Musique*, Dryden revealed the genius of a true poet. And this was enough to make Warton's final ranking inconclusive. His ambivalent assessment of Pope and Dryden revealed the emotional approach to poetry in him vying with the formal, more classical approach. Reason told him to prefer Pope; his heart urged him to choose Dryden. Neither Dryden nor Pope, however, could join the top rank of "true poets." Although, had more of Dryden's work been like his "divine *Musick Ode*" (2:204), Warton would have probably placed him in the highest category.

It is not so much the comparison of the two poets that makes Warton's *Essay* important, but rather his underlying assumption that the species of poetry in which he places Pope and Dryden, that of wit and sense, of the "moral, ethical, and panegyrical," excellent as it may be, still "is not the most excellent one of the art" (1:vii, ii). When Warton called on poetry to return to its true basis in the poet's imagination and its true expression in sublimity and emotion, he linked the already developing idea of the sublime with one that was just beginning to gain ground — the creative imagination.

Philosophers and critics had been searching for ways of viewing man that could better explain the world being revealed by science and its methods. The imagination seemed to provide such ways. James Engell has pointed out that the Great Chain of Being with its static concept of the universe "could no longer take the full brunt of philosophical inquiry." The empirical method and the new sciences which it made possible furthered the break from the past and opened the way for the "dynamic and active" force of the imagination which "more easily explains the interchange of state and the transforming, organic qualities of psyche and nature.[17] By mid-century the creative imagination was just beginning to be developed as a way to "unify man's psyche and, by extension, to reunify man with nature, to return by the paths of self-consciousness to a state of higher nature, a state of the sublime where senses, mind, and spirit elevate the world around them even as they elevate themselves."[18]

From our twentieth-century vantage point, we cannot determine exactly how Warton's *Essay* influenced the literary tastes and aspirations of mid- and late-eighteenth-century England. Certainly, it was well known in literary circles, but because of its diffuseness, readers and critics could respond to the *Essay* in a variety of ways. The three leading literary journals reviewed it, and the *GM* printed several pages of excerpts, or epitomes.[19] Generally the reviewers of both volumes of the *Essay* found it informative, entertaining, and impartial. They said little about Warton's call for reviving "true poetry" or about his placing the century's two poetic giants, Dryden and Pope, in the second rank of poets.

Samuel Johnson wrote the review in the *Literary Magazine*, and he is strangely silent about Warton's placing Pope outside the realm of "true poets." His silence was not consent, however. It must have been in his mind when, some years later he wrote in *The Life of Pope*:

> After all this [examination of Pope's versification] it is surely superfluous to answer the question that has once been asked, Whether Pope was a poet? otherwise than by asking in return If Pope be not a poet, where is poetry to be found? To circumscribe poetry by a definition will only shew the narrowness of the definer, though a definition which shall exclude Pope will not easily be made. Let us look round upon the present time, and back upon the past; let us enquire to whom the voice of mankind has decreed the wreath of poetry; let their productions be examined and their claims stated, and the pretensions of Pope will be no more disputed.[20]

Warton had attempted such a definition — the true poet has "a creative and glowing imagination," and his poetry's primary chararacteristics are the sublime and pathetic — and found Pope wanting. Johnson's practical approach to literature admitted no such definition, except as a revelation of the definer's narrowness. Of the attempt to define poetry, he had originally written more acerbically that it "is the pedantry of a narrow mind" (3:251n).

As we have seen, most of the critics who compared Dryden and Pope found Dryden's poetry more natural and spontaneous than Pope's. Pope was often criticized as being too artificial, as lacking that unpremeditated fire which only natural genius can provide. Those who supported Pope found Dryden's poetry too subject to excess and to gross defects in tone, language and versification. He may have had abundant natural wit, but he lacked artistic judgment and consistency. Samuel Johnson's comparison of the two poets both reflected and extended these ideas.

Samuel Johnson's Comparison

In his *Life of Pope*, Johnson wrote that Dryden's " mind has a larger range." Dryden is more varied but also "capricious," while Pope is "uniform" but also "cautious." Dryden "observes the motions of his own mind; Pope constrains his mind to his own rules of composition" (3:222). Johnson's comparison drew on the traditional paradigms of nature versus art and wit versus judgment. These contrasting pairs paralleled each other with wit being allied to nature because it was God-given and judgment being akin to art because it was learned and capable of improvement. Like critics before him, Johnson applied these terms to distinguish the great but erratic natural genius from the steadier but less sublime artist. Thus Homer was greater than Virgil, Michelangelo than Raphael, and Shakespeare than Jonson.

Although Johnson's comparison of Dryden and Pope conformed to the traditional paradigms, with Dryden possessing more of nature and wit and Pope excelling in art and judgment, his application of these models bore his distinctive mark. He emphasized that, in the greatest literature, nature and art joined as reciprocal partners in a particularly organic way: "Fame cannot spread wide or endure long that is not rooted in nature, and manured by art," and any work which endures "must contain in itself some original principle of growth."[21]

In discussing wit and judgment, Johnson resisted his contemporaries' tendency to restrict wit to a particular kind of mental power. And even when he defined wit more narrowly than general "powers of the mind," he included judgment within it. Conversely, his definition of judgment was broad enough to include contemporary concepts of wit. Judgment both discerned relations and made distinctions. Unlike the usual eighteenth-century view that judgment curbed or corrected wit, Johnson believed it operated somewhat like wit in enhancing an author's depiction of nature rather than retrenching wit's excesses. Thus the

17

relationship of judgment to wit resembled that of art to nature because it used the human ability to think, select, join, and distinguish to enhance, rather than retrench, the poet's native wit.

Johnson's comparison of Dryden and Pope was both traditional and new. Like previous critics, he dwelt on the differences between Dryden's bursts of genius and Pope's steady artistry, but he used a powerful and comprehensive imagery that revivified the old contrasts: "If the flights of Dryden therefore are higher, Pope continues longer on the wing." Dryden's fire blazes brighter; Pope's more regularly. Dryden often astonishes; Pope always delights.[22] Fire and flight fuse with human thought and feeling. Shiels had covered the same ground and had started some of the images; Johnson transformed the comparison as he said Dryden had transformed English poetry, "He found it brick, and he left it Marble."[23]

Where Shiels had examined the poets' works, Johnson explored their minds.[24] Dryden's "mind has the larger range."[25] "The notions of Dryden were formed by comprehensive speculation, and those of Pope by minute attention. There is more dignity in the knowledge of Dryden, and more certainty in that of Pope." Their poetic geniuses differed as wit unbounded differed from wit circumscribed by judgment. Dryden had more of "that energy which collects, combines, amplifies and animates," but "it is not to be inferred that of this poetical vigour Pope had only a little because Dryden had more." Dryden's vigor was intense but sporadic: "What his mind could supply at a call, or gather in one excursion, was all that he sought and all that he gave." Pope's "dilatory caution" led to long and consistent labor "to accumulate all that study might produce, or chance supply." For their prose styles, Johnson turned to the popular eighteenth-century landscape image, with its juxtaposition of nature and art. Dryden's page is a natural field, rising into inequalities, and diversified by the varied exuberance of abundant vegetation; Pope's is a velvet lawn, shaven by the scythe, and levelled by the roller."

Johnson's *Lives of the Poets* was generally well received, although some critics took exception to his harsh treatment of specific poets such as Milton, Gray and Collins. Anna Seward, however, sharply criticized the *Lives* as a whole. She "despised the admirers of Johnson as an equitable critic."[26] She blamed his insensitivity to what she call "the higher walks of poetry" for the "great falling off"[27] in contemporary taste for poets of strong sensibility, which she considered the true index of poetic genius. And, of course, Miss Seward disagreed with Johnson's placing of Pope below Dryden.

18

Most critics, however, considered Johnson's *Lives* of Dryden and Pope to be among his best work. His comparison of the two poets has been quoted repeatedly. The basis for Johnson's comparison was probably familiar to many readers from Shiels's work and, like it, drew on the popular paradigms of nature and art, wit and judgment in language that is among Johnson's most eloquent and humane. If Johnson's *Lives* has "often been taken as a book of wisdom,"[28] the Dryden-Pope comparison strikes most readers as voicing some of its most enduring truths.

Its wisdom still survives, but the paradigms that underlay the comparison were engulfed by the nineteenth century's emphasis on creative imagination and individual expressiveness. The nature and art model had been losing its vitality since the Renaissance. The eighteenth-century kept it alive mainly by linking it with wit and judgment, terms which reflected their concern with the rational mind and its workings. To the Romantic poets, however, these terms represented everything they disliked about the eighteenth century, with its mechanical rules, its love of ornament, its joy in artifice, and its nonorganic compartment-alizing of the human mind. As a paradigm for poetic composition, the interrelation of wit and judgment disappeared.

If Johnson wrote the most memorable eighteenth-century words about Dryden and Pope, he did not write the last. From April 1789 through April 1791, some thirty thousand more were expended in the pages of *The Gentleman's Magazine*. In addition to the two principals, seventeen others joined in the paper war. Most were obscure; a few were well known. Some were temperate; others were vehemently partisan.

THE CONTROVERSIALISTS

The Various Sides

Anna Seward and Joseph Weston were the originators and principal combatants in the controversy about whether Pope or Dryden was the superior poet. Their letters begin and end the debate and occupy most of the space. Weston's letters, which include a transcription of most of the *Preface to the Woodmen of Arden*, fill well over half the space devoted to the controversy. Miss Seward's take up less than a fifth of the space and end midway through the exchange. Weston not only has the last word, but promises more to come. It never does. Of the seventeen other letter writers, six support Miss Seward's position and five side with Weston.

The remainder refute or agree with both sides' arguments, add information of their own, or call for peace. Only twelve of the additional correspondents are included in this text because the other five do not advance the main issues of the controversy, which are the comparison of Dryden and Pope together with related issues of critical theory and method. A list of omitted letters appears at the end of the Textual Introduction.

The unidentified "M. F."[29] is Miss Seward's most prolific champion, contributing six letters to the controversy. "M. F." both supports Miss Seward and attacks Weston, forcing Weston to fight on two fronts at once. "W." (Letter 23), an Edinburgh correspondent, supports Miss Seward's defense of Pope's character. "J. S." (Letter 25) gives learned support to the defense of Pope against Weston's charges in Letter 14 about Pope's treatment of Thomas Burnet and George Duckett.

A particularly scathing attack on Weston comes from "B. L. A." (Letter 28). With a good deal of Greek and Latin fanfare, he undertakes to refute "by chronology" Weston's assertion that Pope "incited Swift to ridicule Dryden in 'The Tale of a Tub.'" The final defense for the Seward camp comes from "Norfolciencis" (Letter 33). Although he is tentatively identified by Kuist as G. Aiken, it seems more likely that he may be John Aikin. There is no record of a G. Aikin in Nichols's *Anecdotes* or *Illustrations*, and Anna Seward's *Letters* do not mention him. John Aikin, however, was practicing medicine in Yarmouth in 1791, and "Norfolciencis's" letter comes from there. Aikin knew Dr. Erasmus Darwin and was known to Anna Seward, who referred to him several times in her *Letters*. She took special notice of Dr. Aikin's interest in poetry.[30] "Norfolciencis" supports "B. L. A.'s" position and reproves those calling for peace by noting that Miss Seward has long since retired from the debate, leaving Weston, like Garrick's Richard III "stabbing the air at the feet of Richmond."

On Weston's side are John Morfitt (Letter 9), whose poem was the occasion for the controversy; "M[arcellu]s" (Henry Francis Cary, Letters 5 and 11); and Philip Thicknesse, (Letter 22) who agrees with Weston about Pope's character. "R. W.," or Bardus Ordovicensis (poet of North Wales) writes from Flintshire in North Wales (Letter 29) supporting Weston.

Among the remainder, "Impartial" (Letter 13) lives up to his pseudonym by agreeing with and praising both Miss Seward and Weston. "R. B." (Letter 30) contributes a brief note commending Pope's wit and Welsted's patience. Calls for peace or at least for silence come from David Dalrymple (Lord Hailes, Letter 31) who also adds some incorrect information about the pamphlet "Homerides;" and "D. R.," who writes in the penultimate letter (34) that "Pope will be read long after he [Weston] will be forgotten."

Individual Backgrounds

Anna Seward (1742-1809) was well known as a poetess, informal essayist, letter writer and literary critic.[31] Although she is usually referred to as "the Swan of Lichfield," no one knows how the epithet originated. Lichfield's proximity to Stratford-upon-Avon may have made Lichfield's citizens think "it should have a Swan, even as Stratford had a hundred years before."[32] We may wonder that the epithet was not attached to a more famous Lichfield native such as Samuel Johnson or David Garrick. That Anna Seward became the Swan of Lichfield attests both to her poetic reputation during her own time as well as to the arresting physical impression she made with her auburn eyes, majestic figure, and melodious voice.

Today we do not read the poetry which made her famous, and we smile at her unceasing enthusiasm conveyed in yards of relentlessly elevated verse. But she was popular in her day for those very qualities. As one *GM* reviewer wrote of her: "There is...a poetess of the age, in whom almost every poetical excellence seems to be united... her merit is so universally acknowledged, that I trust that I shall not be suspected of flattery, even to a female!"[33] By the time the *GM* controversy occurred, she had become "the most famous poetess in England."[34]

One of Anna Seward's earliest and best remembered poems, *Monody on the Death of Major André* (1781), which bitterly denounced his execution as a spy by the Americans, elicited a response from George Washington. A few years after peace had been made, he sent an officer to call on Miss Seward with proofs of Washington's efforts to save André. Washington, the officer assured her, had found no "circumstance of his life...so mortifying as to be censured in the Monody on André."[35] Most of Anna Seward's works were very popular. Her poetical novel *Louisa* (1784) ran to five editions in England and one in America. Her translations of Horace's *Odes*, which were actually paraphrases in verse of English prose translations, appeared regularly in the *GM* during the mid 1780s and were later included in *Original Sonnets on Various Subjects, and Odes Paraphrased from Horace* (1799), which ran to two editions. Although strict scholars criticized them because Miss Seward knew no Latin, others praised them as graceful paraphrases. Their appearance in the *GM* swelled the fame which had been started by her monodies and elegies and continued by *Louisa*. Even Samuel Johnson, her lifelong literary and personal antagonist, had praised a section of her *Elegy on Captain Cook* (1780), which had extended to four editions. Her collection of one hundred of her own sonnets (1799) drew praise from several of the literary journals. In these she is at her best in the minutely observed descriptions of nature. Her *Memoirs of the Life of Dr. Darwin* (1804), although "severely criticised by some reviewers," "remains an eminently readable book," especially the sections about Erasmus Darwin's life, personality, and friends.[36] After her death, *The Beauties of Anna Seward*[37] continued her fame into the first quarter of the nineteenth century.

Anna Seward was a prolific letter writer and shows to advantage in this form. Her letters still provide eighteenth-century researchers with information about a wide variety of literary figures. The biographers of people as diverse as Henry Francis Cary and Maria Edgeworth quote her extensively.[38] The six volumes of letters which she chose for publication are by her own reckoning "only a twelfth part of what she had written."[39] Inflated enthusiasms, stilted diction, and verbosity mar some of her letters, especially those to authors or critics whom she wanted to impress. But even parts of these letters, together with others to humbler recipients, show her more direct and sensible side. Although too often carried away by enthusiasm for the poets of her time, she could be a sharp critic and judge of both literature and people. When she allowed herself to speak frankly and without embellishment, her opinions are worth reading.

She loved to talk and argue about poets and poetry. Of the four controversies published in the *GM* in which she was involved, three revolve around this favorite topic, and the fourth concerns the related topic of pulpit oratory. She believed passionately in the progress of poetry. She read her contemporaries, good and bad alike, with pleasure and pride. Her third list of poets, those of the "modern" period which began with Pope's death in 1744 (Letters 1a and 1b) shows her overwhelming, if undiscriminating, preference for her contemporaries. Of the more than fifty contemporary poets she hailed as the geniuses of her day, less than a dozen are still read with any frequency. Many of the remainder have been relegated to the ranks of what she called "pretenders" and "poetasters" (Letter 1a), from which she felt her lists to be free. Indeed, the poet she names second (after Gray) is William Hayley, whose works have long been consigned to the poetaster trash heap. Her inclusion of Thomson and Collins in the modern period is questionable, because their dates (1700-1748 and 1721-1759 respectively) place them in Pope's time.[40] She admits her mistake with Thomson, but defends

Collins's placement because his fame came after mid-century (Letter 7).

At the time the Pope-Dryden controversy began, Anna Seward was forty-seven. She lived with her seriously ill father in the bishop's palace (former home of Gilbert Walmesley, mentor of the young Johnson and Garrick) in Lichfield's Cathedral Close. As the daughter of Canon Thomas Seward, Anna was socially and economically secure. She played a central role in Lichfield society not only because of her position but also because of her personality. People liked her and enjoyed her company. Her fame as a poetess was increasing and would increase further. Her circle included Dr. Erasmus Darwin, author of the *Botanic Garden* (1789-1791) and grandfather of Charles Darwin; Lucy Porter, Samuel Johnson's step-daughter; Richard Lovell Edgeworth, father of Maria Edgeworth; Thomas Day, author of *Sandford and Merton* (1783-1786), a didactic novel for children which contained advanced theories about child-rearing and education; and the youthful Henry Francis Cary, translator of Dante. Dr. Darwin had encouraged her early verse writing and she subsequently composed some seventy lines of verse on his actual botanic garden which was printed in the *GM* in 1783 and which Darwin appropriated for the exordium to his *Botanic Garden.*[41] Although she opposed most of Johnson's opinions about poetry and deplored his rough treatment of those whom he considered intellectually inferior and pretentious (including Miss Seward's father), she knew him all her life and visited him often during the closing months of his life.

Anna Seward was passionately fond of music, especially Handel. Lichfield choirmaster, John Saville, was her dear friend (some even said lover, but this is doubtful). Her acquaintance with Joseph Weston began through Saville and was probably furthered by his being an organist. In a sense Anna Seward was also a musical performer. She was often asked to read poetry (her own or others') aloud, and her voice was so musical that wherever she went she was asked to perform. Her own poetry benefited greatly from her fine reading in which tone and expression masked poetic shortcomings.

Her world extended beyond Lichfield. William Hayley, arbiter of literary taste and thought by many to be the leading poet of his day, was her friend and literary comrade for much of her life. She met and corresponded with a number of literary figures, including Sir Walter Scott, Robert Southey, Hannah More, Helen Maria Williams, and Hester Thrale. The advocate of abolition, William Wilberforce, visited her, as did Thomas Erskine, the famous Whig orator who became Lord Chancellor. Dr. Samuel Parr, who was, in Hesketh Pearson's words, "a sort of whig Dr. Johnson,"[42] called on her. Romney painted her. Scott sent her his early works for comment and edited her literary remains, which included his memoir of her and extracts from her letters.

As a critic and arbiter of taste, she was listened to and respected, as the contributors to the controversy all attest. Joseph Weston is guilty of less hyperbole than we might at first think in calling her "one of the finest Writers of the Age" (Letter 4).

Joseph Weston (c. 1743-c. 1825) was an organist in the small town of Solihull, a few miles southeast of Birmingham. His humble origin and general obscurity probably added to his apprehension about debating with Anna Seward. As she notes, "He was by no means calculated to the meridian of our pompous gentry."[43] Anna Seward's letters provide most of our information about him. Her vivid description of the comic yet intellectually impressive figure he cut not only gives us a distinct picture of Weston but also shows how direct and lively she can be when she descends from her Parnassian elevation:

> ... his height and proportion mighty slender, and well enough by nature, but fidgeted and noddled into an appearance not over prepossessing; nor are his sharp features and very sharp little eyes a whit behind them in quizzity. Then he is drest — ye gods, how he is drest! — in a salmon-coloured coat, sattin waistcoat, and small-clothes of the same warm aurora-tint. ... A hat furiously cocked and pinched, too small in the crown to admit his head, sticks upon the extremest summit of the full-winged caxon [wig]. ... He talks down the hours, but knows nothing of their flight.

But, she continues: "His wit, intelligence, and poetic genius are a mine," and his "taste and real accuracy in criticism" are clear. Finally, the "heart of this ingenious and oddly compounded being, is open, ardent, and melting as even female-tenderness."[44] The peculiarities which Miss Seward noticed on first meeting Weston show in the letters he writes during the controversy. He is hyper-sensitive and verbose. His nervous prose is studded with italics, capitals, and dashes. Yet he appears to have read almost as much as Miss Seward, and remembers it more accurately. He catches her several times in her frequent practice of imprecise quotation.

At the time of the controversy, Weston had published a few poems in the *GM*, including one to Miss Seward's young protegés Henry Francis Cary and Thomas Lister.[45] He had translated John Morfitt's *Philotoxi Ardenae* (1788) into blank verse and Drydenic couplets. To this he added as preface "An Essay on the Superiority of Dryden's Versification over that of *Pope* and of the *Moderns*," which started the controversy. This is his only work to extend to a second edition (1885). In the early 1790s, the

GM published several patriotic poems in which Weston deplored Napoleonic France's "tyrant Liberty and anarch laws."[46] Preoccupation with the events in France may explain Weston's failure to finish his proofs of Pope's villainous character. He continued his connection with the Lichfield circle at least through 1793 when he wrote an "Occasional Prologue, *For the Opening of the New Theatre, Lichfield.*"[47] In it, he describes a "drop scene" with a statue of Shakespeare bearing medallions on its pedestal which picture Miss Seward, Dr. Johnson, and Mr. Garrick. With undiminished gallantry, he refers to Anna Seward as "The bright-ey'd Champion of mellifluous Pope."

In addition to his connection with Lichfield literary society, Weston seems to have mingled to some extent in Birmingham literary society. His name is joined with Birmingham resident John Morfitt's in two of his three published works, both of which were published in Birmingham. At some time during his life, probably after the Pope-Dryden controversy, he became a close friend of the Suffolk peasant poet Robert Bloomfield.[48] He edited the poet's *Remains* (1824) and in his preface called Bloomfield, "one of the most perfect poets of his day" (viii). He admired the "extreme purity of his taste" and sounded a Johnsonian note in remarking that, "his rural scenes are never infested with dryads, or fauns, or genii, or any other phantoms of foreign extraction" (ix). The defender of Dryden's "full resounding Line" and "long, majestic march" (*2HEI* 4:268-69) apparently became attracted to the "simple and unaffected"[49] style of Romantic nature poetry. In his prefatory essay and during the controversy, Weston calls for a return to a simpler style. At some point he stopped looking for models in the past and began finding them in the present. His individual movement from the cause of Drydenic purity to that of Romantic rusticity unites him with the great revolution in poetic taste that was taking place even as the paper war about Dryden and Pope extended through 24 issues of the *GM*. Whatever his faults as a critic, he saw what was coming sooner than many and devoted himself as zealously to the Romantic cause as he had to the Drydenic.

Henry Francis Cary (1772-1844) was a schoolboy of fifteen at the time of the controversy. He grew up to become "the greatest Italian scholar of his age."[50] His translation of Dante, initially made famous by Coleridge's lectures, has, according to the *DNB*, "remained the translation which, on Dante's name being mentioned, occurs first to the mind." Cary first attracted Anna Seward's notice through the poetry he contributed to the *GM* in 1787. His close friend and fellow-poet, Thomas Lister, who lived just outside Lichfield, had also drawn Miss Seward's notice. Through Lister, Cary met Miss Seward in the spring of 1788 and "was enrolled among her disciples and adorers."[51] Cary's biographer deplores the "Sewardian" influence on Cary's early poetry, which consists of odes and sonnets, most of which were ornate and sentimental, together with translations of a number of Horace's odes, some Greek pieces and one Italian poem. Despite his great admiration for the Swan of Lichfield, Cary had an independent mind and showed it in the letters he wrote as "M — — s" (short for his adopted poetic name "Marcellus"[52]) while still her devoted protegé. He disagreed with Miss Seward about her three lists of poets and about her criticism of Dryden's unpruned and weedy "wilderness" (Letter 1c). With the glee of a student tripping up his mentor, he turned the metaphor to Dryden's support. Dryden rendered his "poetic garden... spacious" rather "nicely beautiful." Weeds did mingle with his flowers, but he preferred Dryden's "wilderness" to Pope's "elegant parterres" (Letter 11).

Miss Seward gives no indication that she recognizes Cary's hand in the "M — — s" letters. In her letters to him, she is quick to correct what seem to her to be his errors in poetic taste, but the letters from this period contain no mention of the controversy. As Cary matured, he left the Seward fold and devoted himself to the exact and unostentatious form of translation for which he is still known.

John Morfitt (c. 1740-1809) had a good deal in common with his translator Joseph Weston. They both admired Dryden, feared the menace of the French Revolution and Napoleon's imperialism, and used their literary talents to express their patriotism. Like Weston, he was relatively obscure and is known to us primarily through the letters of Anna Seward, to whom he sent a copy of *The Woodmen of Arden*. Morfitt was a barrister at law in Birmingham, where he took an active part in public affairs. He wrote essays on legal matters affecting Birmingham and exhorted his countrymen to patriotic efforts during the Napoleonic wars.

Philip Thicknesse (1719-1792) spent most of his adult life in military or government service. Plain-spoken and contentious, he combined great integrity and generosity with "the faculty of lessening the number of his friends and increasing the number of his enemies" (*DNB*). His quixotic behavior affected his entire life, causing him to change residences often, and even to exile himself in Spain after losing a lawsuit. His diverse and numerous writings include comments on man-midwifery, an eight-volume biography of Thomas Gainsborough, and accounts of his travels in Europe, Jamaica, and Georgia.

Sir David Dalrymple, Lord Hailes (1726-1792), was a renowned Scottish judge, scholar, and author. His knowledge of legal history equaled that of his distinguished contemporary Lord Monboddo. He was acquainted with many of the leading thinkers and writers of his day, including Johnson, Boswell, Burke, Hume and Adam Smith. A judicious and broad-minded judge, he was "distinguished for humanity at a time when the criminal bench was disgraced by opposite qualities" (*DNB*).

As the magazine that would publish 30,000 words of debate about two deceased poets without fear of losing its readers, the *GM* is a peculiarly eighteenth-century phenomenon. Its origin and nature bear looking at in more detail.

The Gentleman's Magazine

The Gentleman's Magazine was the first and longest-lived periodical of its kind. When the Pope-Dryden controversy began, it was 58 years old and destined to continue publication for more than another century, finally ceasing in 1922. Founded by printer Edward Cave in 1731, it began as a miscellaneous collection of articles reprinted or digested from other sources to make it easy to keep up with "all the News-Papers (which of late are so multiplied as to render it impossible, unless a Man makes it a Business, to consult them all)" and also provide "some other Matters of Use or Amusement that will be communicated to us."[53]

But, the *GM* was more than just an eighteenth-century *Readers' Digest*. Even before it began including original material, it attempted to cover the current history of its day, and it soon grew into a periodical which combined the features of today's *Time*, *U.S. News and World Report*, *The New York Times Book Review*, *The New Yorker*, *National Geographic*, *Science Digest* and *The Farmer's Almanac*.

Edited by the fictitious Sylvanus Urban, whose name comprehended both country and city, it was intended for a large and varied audience. Its monthly issues covered national and foreign affairs; births, marriages and deaths of emminent persons, ecclesiastical appointments, political debates, bankruptcy notices, grain prices, gardening notes, and advice from the farrier. It soon added poetry and book reviews, and from 1735 on also depended increasingly on correspondence from its readers. Albert Pailler estimates that during Cave's time the *GM* had between six and seven hundred correspondents and that most of them submitted only one piece.[54] This dependence on its readers as contributors fostered the close connections between reader-authors and the *GM*'s editor which continued throughout Nichols's tenure as editor (he died in 1826) and was a major factor in keeping the Pope-Dryden debate going for two years.

The *GM*'s original title indicates the breadth of its potential audience: *The Gentleman's Magazine; or Trader's Monthly Intelligencer*. The rather touchingly explicit "Trader's" was dropped after the first issue, but its audience remained much broader than even its original name implied. It comprised the landed gentry (both male and female), manufacturers, clergymen, scholars, governesses, office clerks, and soldiers.

Because of its wide appeal together with Cave's industry and good management, the *GM* prospered. In addition to contributions from readers, which cost nothing, Cave employed a number of excellent professional writers and editors, the most outstanding being Samuel Johnson. For about seven years from 1738 on, Johnson was also probably the *GM*'s chief editor and a key figure in making the magazine far more intellectual than it had been at its outset.[55] Cave's sense of what made news, together with his interest in science let him to publish the first report of Benjamin Franklin's *Experiments and Observations in Electricity*, after the Royal Society had "barely condescended" to notice it.[56]

Although many imitators sprang up in the wake of the *GM*'s success, Cave kept his magazine ahead of the competition. His figures for 1746 show a circulation of 3,000 copies a month, a very large one for the time, and one which presumably increased throughout the remainder of the century. When Cave died, he left behind a well-established magazine that "was within the next century destined to become one of the most important influences on literature and on the reading of persons of all classes."[57]

A few years before the Pope-Dryden controversy, Nichols expanded the *GM* had expanded in coverage and size. With the 53rd volume (1783), it began appearing in two parts, each of almost 600 pages each as contrasted with the previous year's single 600-page volume. In 1790, the *GM*'s fictional editor, Mr. Urban, proudly reported his magazine and its staff "to stand conspicuous in the foremost rank of Monthly Journalists," where they functioned as "the brief, but faithful, reporters of the Chronicle of the Times" (3:lxvii).

The Pope-Dryden controversy involved two things which the *GM* had always featured — poetry and Pope. From its early years, the *GM* had published poetry. As was true of all the magazines during the 1730s and 40s, the verse was second or third rate, "without individualized expression or original talent," and revealing all too clearly "the inward decay of Neo-Classicism."[58] Most of the verse was short mostly occasional. It was often contributed by readers, and, like everything else in the magazine, it was calculated for wide public appeal. Because of this, as Lennart Carlson notes, the *GM* "is still valuable as an index to the tastes of an an age."[59]

The *GM* did publish some first-rate poetry, but almost always as lengthy extracts from an established author's works such as Pope's *Essay on Man*, which was extracted at length. Pope himself was the single most frequently quoted poet during Cave's time. During Nichols's editorship, the poetry section ("Poetical Essays") continued Cave's tradition of short unremarkable pieces revealing none of the ferment that was about to produce the Romantic revolution. The blandness of the poetry contrasted with the fierce debates published in the "Prose Essay" section.

The Pope-Dryden controversy was one of the keenest and shows how Nichols managed the *GM* as a literary forum. By publishing the letters from the two principals, Weston and Seward, in installments and dividing them at provocative junctures, while simultaneously feeding in contributions from other combatants at strategic intervals, Nichols kept his readers eagerly awaiting each monthly issue. This practice angered some of the correspondents, especially when letters were held for a long time or when dates were changed, as with "M.F.'s" first letter which was actually written before Anna Seward's first letter. According to Nichols's note,[60] the date was changed by accident. Although it is not clear when the letter was received, it could well have arrived before Anna Seward's, but didn't capture Nichols's interest until after he saw hers. Anna Seward was well-known to the *GM*'s readers as a poetess as well as a lively controversialist (the first four letters in her debate with Boswell and others about Samuel Johnson had appeared just two years earlier), and her long, wide-ranging letter promised to capture readers' interest more securely than the unknown "M.F.'s." Whether "M.F.'s" letter was accidentally or purposely delayed, the result was better for circulation.

THE ISSUES

The debate centered on the main issues of Pope's character and the value of his poetry, especially its effect on his successors. Weston charged Pope with inveterate vindictiveness to a whole range of victims, especially poets. The principal argument about this comes down to whether Pope intentionally stigmatized Thomas Burnet and George Duckett as homosexuals. Pope seems to have had good reason to dislike both men. They had happily publicized his accidental connection with treason in his publication of Buckingham's *Works* (1723) and had attempted to undercut translation of the *Iliad* in the pamphlet *Homerides* (1716), which they originally and maliciously titled *The Hump Conference* (1715). Although Pope's animosity toward Burnet and Duckett seems justified,

29

his method of paying them off in *The Dunciad* may be questioned. Pope was more powerful with pen and innuendo than they, and his verses in *Dunciad* (A) slid the stiletto and the notes gave it a brutal twist. Duckett "is said to have demanded and obtained satisfaction from Pope"[61] for the implications of homosexuality in these lines and the scurrilous epigram in the notes. Pope's own notes to the passage in *Dunciad* (A) show he was aware of its implication. John Dennis had drawn the inference, and Pope quotes his interpretation at length in order to deny its truth.[62] The Twickenham editors note that "Pope may have been sincere in his protestations; but he never suppressed the passage, nor the note calling attention to Dennis's interpretation of it" (5:3.176n). In *Dunciad* (B), Pope ommitted the lines containing the names and deleted the epigram (5:3.179-84 and note), but in his note to the lines he reminded the reader of the previous version. Weston is certainly right that the compliments are insults and the epigram is scurrilous, and Pope tacitly admitted this by his modifications in both *Dunciad* (A) and (B). But, in the pamphlet wars few holds were barred, and Burnet and Duckett had struck first.

Pope's defenders in the controversy struggle to clear him of all scandalous intent. "M.F." takes up the Pope side, because Miss Seward, as a lady, cannot be imagined to understand or take part in such a debate. Weston sees Pope as an inveterate monster of malice, but in the end his arguments grow shrill and repetitive, doing his cause more harm than good.

Weston's complaints about Pope's poetry center around what he saw as Pope's obsessive correctness, his monotonously regular couplets, and above all his overly refined poetic diction. In contrast to this, Weston applauded Dryden's variety, exuberance, and energy. Even Dryden's "flats" in thought and expression were deliberate: "He, therefore *subdued* his Style *occasionally* — to burst upon his Reader with *greater Splendour*, when the Subject demanded a Loftier Lay" (Letter 8c). Discussing this point in Letter 8d, Weston cites a passage from Joseph Warton's *Essay* which says in part that Dryden's practice was "sometimes to soften and subdue his tints, and not to paint and adorn every Object he touched, with Perpetual Pomp, and unremitted Splendor."[63] Weston charges that Pope's over-refinement had a devastating effect on his successors, whose Pope-inspired obsession with brilliance led them to "torture [poetry] into *Obscurity*, and refine [it] into *Imbecility*" (Letter 8c).

To this Anna Seward counters, in Letter 1b, by attacking Dryden. She cites his "incongruous metaphor, inconsistent fable, and prating familiarity of expression" as well as his poorly placed Alexandrines and "botching" triplets (7, 10). Although prepared to defend Pope's versification, she sees it as a minor part of his or any author's poetry because:

> A poem has little merit if it does not remain fine poetry after having been taken out of *all* measure. Where there is loftiness of thought, ingenuity of allusion, and strength of imagery, to stand *that* test, true lovers of the art allow an author to do almost what he pleases with the numbers, provided he does not insist upon their preference of the slovenly to the polished ones, readily promising that such a work shall be dear to them in *any* dress
>
> (Letter 1c).

At first glance we might take this for a revolutionary poetic manifesto, with its suggestion that the poet's thought and expression are the core of his poem and that the form is shaped by them. But Miss Seward soft pedals the revolutionary tone with her proviso that the numbers be "polished." Polish to her, as to William Hayley and the other poetasters whom she admired, was just what it sounds like — laid on from the outside and the more the better. Polish, along with ornament, was the second-rate poet's downfall. Also, Anna Seward's dictum overlooks what makes Pope's poetry great — stunningly successful integration of thought and feeling with sound and rhythm.

The debate narrows down to what Weston had written in the Preface (most of which he reproduces in Letter 8c) about Pope's influence on poetic diction: "Let me not be misunderstood. — Poetic Diction, and that Alone, is the Object of my Reprobation." Weston argues that poetic diction has seriously declined since Dryden's time, largely because of Pope's influence; Seward maintains that under Pope's influence, it has improved. Weston contrasts Dryden's simplicity, variety, and unaffected sublimity with the "*modern* System" which "appears decisively to exclude every Mode of Expression from *Poetry* which is so unlucky as to find a Place in *Prose*." As examples of the new poetic diction he cites, "harsh Construction and fantastic Inversion — Tinsel Phrases and tinkling Compound-Epithets."

Anna Seward is firmly rooted in the eighteenth-century outlook regarding poetic diction. Like Johnson, she decries using low or common expressions and approves of elegance. But unlike Johnson she too often confuses lowness with simplicity and ludicrous inflation with elegance. In Letter 15, she gives her improved translation of Juno's speech in Book I of the *Aeneid*. Her version makes Dryden's clear and forceful language turgid and weak. Dryden's "Cou'd[64] angry Pallas, with revengeful spleen,/ The Grecian navy burn, and drown the men?" becomes, "Shall

[handwritten margin note: The debate comes down to a disagreement over poetic diction.]

31

injur'd Pallas, with avenging aim,/ O'erwhelm the Greeks, and wrap their fleets in flame?" Such revisions underscore what Weston was objecting to: second-rate poets (and poetesses) who thought they were carrying on Pope's tradition when they were actually bedizening poetry with tinsel phrases.

Anna Seward talks about poetry better than she writes it. Her general principles seem unexceptionable. She agrees with Weston's quotation from Joseph Warton in praise of Dryden's use of "common and familiar words" (Letter 8d). Although Warton's comment "perfectly meets [Miss Seward's] sentiments," she will not allow it to apply to the passage from the *Aeneid* because there the common words do not suit the character of the speaker" (Letter 15). For Anna Seward a goddess is an elevated being who must always speak in elevated language.

In his dissatisfaction with contemporary poetry, Joseph Weston partially anticipates the kind of stand Wordsworth takes only a decade later. Whatever the accuracy of his critical insights, however, Weston is neither the poet nor revolutionary theorist that Wordsworth is. In looking backward for a fixed model and insisting that simply a change in poetic diction and versification can refresh poetry, he recommends an external cure for an internal disease. He wants to fight the stultifying effects of Pope's correctness with a correctness of his own.

Both Anna Seward and Joseph Weston applauded the works of the poets who would eventually help bring about the Romantic revolution. But neither of them had the philosophic grounding or aesthetic insight to describe their appreciation of Romantic poetry in terms that go much beyond enthusiastic exclamation.

Despite its shortcomings as literary criticism, the controversy gives us some insights into how literary debate was carried on among the members of polite society in eighteenth-century England. It also reveals some things about what we now call sexual politics. Combat with "the Swan of Litchfield" upsets Joseph Weston. His illness during the first summer of the controversy may well have been aggravated or even caused by the debate. His hyper-sensitivity leads him to conduct his side of the conflict with an uneasy combination of sugary flattery and bitter acrimony. He does not hesitate to brand Pope as devious, self-serving, and "execrable," while simultaneously addressing Pope's ardent defender, Anna Seward, as a "Thalestris" who "discovers a countenance that melts down all opposition, and eyes that dim the radiance of the gems that spangle-o'er her burnished helmet" (Letter 4).

As the debate warms up, Weston's chivalry suffers. Despite his initial delicacy in refusing to discuss Burnet and Duckett's imputed homosexuality in a letter to Miss Seward, he presents all the details in his letter to "M. F." which he sends to the *GM* for all to read. He also levels some telling sarcasms at his bright-eyed Thalestris's diction. Discussing her rewriting of Dryden's description of Juno's wrath, he notes her translation is neither faithful to the original in Virgil's *Aeneid*, nor is it good poetry (Letter 21). With a subtle irony worthy of Jane Austen, he notes:

> The chief Blemish in *modern* poetic Diction is Inflation. If that Blemish is undiscoverable in Miss Seward's Works, it is probably owing to the Grandeur and Sublimity of her Conceptions, which *justify* the uniform Majesty of her Style. The *Shortness* of her Poems is a Circumstance also much in her Favour.

Anna Seward has an easier job of managing her tone. She is not obliged to be elaborately and artificially polite to her opponent while demolishing his arguments. Thus she manages to sound more sincere and balanced, more "masculine," than Weston.

Weston commits the very sins of which he accuses Pope in his Preface: attempting "to undermine the Reputation of the deceased Poet, and to asperse the Characters of his living Supporters" (Letter 8c). While charging Pope with using "Means not very *honourable*" to undermine Dryden's reputation and place himself on the throne, Weston himself uses the questionable tactic of making a damning accusation and withholding the proof. He never produces the "Work" he has held so long which, would render "Pope's *Goodness of Heart* . . . no longer *problematical*."

Perhaps the most striking feature of the debate is the importance which the controversialists ascribe to poetry and the time they are willing to spend reading and writing about it. In part this reflects their more leisured era. But reading and talking about poetry was far more central to their time than to ours. Yet, even today, we share their concern with what makes writing effective. And we share their fascination with how an author's character influences his work.

As the controversy dwindled down to Weston's single combat against a variety of Pope supporters, Nichols called a halt to contributions from everyone except Miss Seward and Joseph Weston. Even after this, he printed letters from five correspondents besides Weston, one of them being from David Dalrymple, Lord Hailes. But interest was waning. Anna Seward had dropped out of the debate six months earlier (her last letter apeared in the June 1790 issue). Weston was repeating himself and others without producing "Pope's Evidence Against Himself" (Letter 35). In a note to this letter, Nichols declined to insert anything further except another letter from Weston which Nichols noted "is to appear in our next," but does not. We cannot tell if there was such a letter or if Nichols was just holding out bait. If the letter existed and was just more of the same, Nichols probably decided that his readers would stand no more. And so, the twenty-four month talk show was over.

THE TEXT

Editing and Arrangement of the Letters

I have edited the letters to focus on the principal issues of the controversy: the comparison of Dryden and Pope and related issues in literary theory and criticism. Five of the letters contributed nothing new to these issues, so I have omitted them. A chronological list of those letters appears at the end this introduction. Other letters, especially those from Joseph Weston, contain irrelevant or repetitive sections. I have omitted those sections and indicated and their absence by four asterisks (* * * *). Sometimes, I have given brief summaries of the omitted sections; these are enclosed in square brackets.

The letters are numbered consecutively in the order in which they appeared in *The Gentleman's Magazine*. This does not always correspond to their dates. The *GM* usually printed the long letters from Anna Seward and Joseph Weston when they were received or, if they were too long for a single issue, in consecutive issues. Letters from other correspondents were not always printed when received, but were sometimes held for several months.

Reproduction of the Letters

I have preserved the spelling, punctuation, and capitalization of the originals in the *GM*. I have modernized the eighteenth-century's long "s." Typographical limitations do not allow reproduction of the large and small capital letters often employed in the eighteenth century for proper names and emphasis; therefore, I have used only initial capitals. I have been unable to reproduce the elided "Ae" as in Aeneas.

I have followed modern practice of indenting long quotations, but I have reproduced the quotation marks as printed in the *GM*. I have reproduced quotations in foreign languages exactly as they appeared in the *GM*, because it is not possible to ascertain from which text the writer is quoting.

I have collated the quotations from Dryden and Pope with the standard twentieth-century editions (James Kinsley's edition of Dryden's poetry and the Twickenham edition of Pope's poetry). I have noted all the variations in wording but not in accidentals such as spelling, capitalization, italics, and punctuation. Corrections of short misquotations appear in brackets in the text. Longer ones appear in footnotes. Illegible words which I have deciphered from the context are followed by a question mark in brackets [?]. I have put corrections of obvious printing errors in brackets.

Annotation of the Letters

Notes to the letters, either by the author or the *GM*'s editor, appear at the end of the particular letter. The *GM*'s editor identified his note by an asterisk or a dagger. To keep these straight when there is more than one such note to a letter, I have added another asterisk or dagger to each successive note (for the second note, ** or ††; for the third, *** or †††, and so on). My own notes begin at the end of the letters. In the letter from "B.L.A." (No. 28), the writer used arabic numerals. To distinguish his notes from mine, I have enclosed his footnote numbers in parentheses. When a *GM* footnote has called for annotation, I have added my note to it, enclosed in square brackets.

The correspondents quoted freely from each other's letters. Often they transposed words, changed verb tenses or form, and otherwise adjusted the original to fit into their own writing. I have not noted such alterations unless they changed the meaning of the original.

I have followed the revised (1984) *MLA Handbook*'s form for annotation. Its most significant changes are omitting "p." and "pp." before page numbers, and abbreviating publishers' names: e.g.: UP = University Press, Holt = Holt, Rinehart, and Winston.

For frequently cited works, I have used short titles, a list of which follows. All references to Pope's poetry are to *The Twickenham Edition of the Poems of Alexander Pope*, ed. John Butt, *et. al.*, 11 vols. (London: Methuen, 1961-1969). All references to Dryden's poetry are to *The Poems of John Dryden*, ed. James Kinsley, 4 vols. (Oxford: Clarendon, 1958). In the text of the letters, references to Dryden's and Pope's poetry appear in brackets following each quotation. They are in this order: title, volume, book or part if appropriate, and line(s). For example [*Il* 8:23.141-49.] refers to Pope's *Iliad*, Twickenham edition volume 8, book 23, lines 141-49. In the case of volumes with several parts, the volume number is separated from the part number by a period (e.g., 3.2 is volume three, part two).

I have used the *New Cambridge Bibliography of English Literature* as the authority for publication information, and where that is incomplete or unclear, the *British Museum Catalogue*. For biographical information, I have used the *Dictionary of National Biography*, unless otherwise noted. Definitions from Samuel Johnson's *Dictionary* are from the 1755 edition.

I have used the Loeb Classical Library editions for the following authors: Cicero, Horace, Livy, Ovid, Plutarch, Seneca, and Virgil.

Letters Omitted from This Text

Joseph Weston, *GM* 59.2:780.
Joseph Weston, *GM* 60.1:160-63.
Joseph Weston, *GM* 60.1:196.
M[atthew] G[reen], *GM* 60.2:905-06.
Obadiah Meanwell, *GM* 60.2:1006-07.
Maria, *GM* 60.2:1097-98.
L.M., "Sonnet," *GM* 60.2:1132.
Remigius, *GM* 60.2:1193.

SHORT TITLES AND ABBREVIATIONS

Abbreviations of Dryden's and Pope's poems correspond to those used in the concordances: Guy Montgomery, ed., *Concordance to the Poetical Works of John Dryden* (Los Angeles: U of California P, 1957); Emmett G. Bedford and Robert J. Dilligan, eds., *A Concordance to the Poems of Alexander Pope*, 2 vols. (Detroit: Gail Research Co., 1974).

Ae = *The Aeneid*, Dryden.

AF = *Alexander's Feast; or The Power of Musique. An Ode, In Honour of St. Cecilia's Day*, Dryden.

$Arbu$ = *An Epistle from Mr. Pope, to Dr. Arbuthnot*, Pope.

CA = Ovid's *Metamorphoses, Ceyx and Alcyone*, Dryden.

DA = Ovid's *Epistles, Dido to Aeneas*, Dryden.

DNB = *Dictionary of National Biography*.

Dramatic Poesy = John Dryden, *Of Dramatic Poesy and Other Critical Essays*, ed. George Watson, 2 vols. (London: Dent, 1962).

$DunA$ = *The Dunciad* (A), Pope.

$DunB$ = *The Duncaid* (B), Pope.

$ElAb$ = *Eloisa to Abelard*, Pope.

EOC = *An Essay on Criticism*, Pope.

$Ep1$ = *Epistle I, To Sir Richard Temple, Lord Viscount Cobham*, Pope.

$Ep2$ = *Epistle II, To a Lady. Of the Characters of Women*, Pope.

$Ep3$ = *Epistle III, To Allan Lord Bathurst*, Pope.

$Ep4$ = *Epistle IV, to Richard Boyle, Earl of Burlington*, Pope.

EOM = *An Essay on Man*, Pope.

EpJ = *Epistle to Mr. Jervas*, Pope.

GM = *The Gentleman's Magazine*, vols. 1-63 (1730-1793).

HAP = *The Hind and the Panther*, Dryden.

2HE1 = *Horatian Epistle, Book 2, Epistle 1*, Pope.

HP = Ovid's *Epistles, Helen to Paris*, Dryden.

HS2 = *Horatian Satire, Book 2, Satire 2*, Pope.

Il = *The Iliad*, Pope.

Johnson, *Works* = *The Yale Edition of the Works of Samuel Johnson*, various editors, vols. 1-10, 14-15 (New Haven: Yale UP, 1958-1985).

Kinsley = The Poems of John Dryden (see p. cxxix for full reference).

Letters = *The Letters of Anna Seward: Written between the Years 1784 and 1807*, ed. A. Constable, 6 vols. (Edinburgh: G. Ramsay, 1811).

Lives = *Johnson's Lives of the English Poets*, ed. G. B. Hill, 3 vols. (Oxford: Clarendon, 1905).

Lives 1 = *Life of Dryden*;

Lives 2 = *Life of Addison*;

Lives 3 = *Life of Pope* or *Life of Gray*.

Mack, *Life* = Maynard Mack, *Alexander Pope: A Life* (New Haven: Yale UP, 1985).

Od = *The Odyssey*, Pope.

OED = *Oxford English Dictionary* (1970).

NCBEL = *New Cambridge Bibliography of English Literature*.

PWi = *The Pastorals, Winter*, Pope.

SG = *Sigismonda and Guiscardo, from Boccace*, Dryden.

TJD = *To My Honour'd Kinsman, John Driden*, Dryden.

TF = *The Temple of Fame*, Pope.

Twk = *The Twickenham Edition of the Poems of Alexander Pope* (see p. 50 for full reference).

UDH = *Upon the Death of the Lord Hastings*, Dryden.

VP4 = *Virgil's Pastorals, The Fourth Pastoral. or, Pollio*, Dryden.

WA = *The Woodmen of Arden* from the Latin of John Morfitt with "An Essay on the Superiority of Dryden's Versification over that of *Pope* and of the *Moderns*," by Joseph Waeston (Birmingham, 1788).

Warton, *Essay* = Joseph Warton, *An Essay on the Genius and Writings of Pope*, 2 vols. (London, 1806).

TABLE OF LETTERS

Ltr.	*GM* Vol.	Issue	*GM* Page	Author	Letter Date
1a	59.1	April	291-92	Seward	Apr. 25, 1789
1b	59.1	May	389-91	Seward	Apr. 25, 1789
1c	59.1	June	510-12	Seward	Apr. 25, 1789
2	59.1	June	512	M. F.	May 30, 1789
3	59.2	July	583	Weston	Jul. 20, 1789
4	59.2	Aug.	680-82	Weston	Aug. 23, 1789
5	59.2	Aug.	682-83	M[arcellu]s	Aug. 5, 1789
6	59.2	Sept.	818	M. F.	Sept. 8, 1789
7	59.2	Sept.	818	Seward	Sept. 15, 1789
8a	59.2	Oct.	875-76	Weston	Oct. 26, 1789
8b	59.2	Nov.	971-72	Weston	Oct. 26, 1789
8c	59.2	Dec.	1101-06	Weston	Nov. 23, 1789
8d	60.1	Jan.	26-33	Weston	Nov. 23, 1789
9	60.1	Jan.	6-7	Morfitt	Jan. 11, 1790
10	60.1	Feb.	118-20	Seward	Feb. 13, 1790
11	60.1	Feb.	120-21	M[arcellu]s	Oct. 11, 1789
12	60.1	Feb.	122-23	M. F.	Oct. 14, 1789
13	60.1	Feb.	123	Impartial	Oct. 31, 1789
14	60.1	May	386-88	Weston	Apr. 25, 1790
15	60.1	June	523-25	Seward	June 16, 1790
16	60.2	July	583-84	M. F.	Jan. 15, 1790
17	60.2	July	697-98	M.F.	Feb. 8, 1790
18	60.2	Sept.	777-80	Weston	Sept. 25, 1790
19	60.2	Sept.	786-87	M. F.	June 15, 1790
20	60.2	Oct.	903-05	Weston	Oct. 11, 1790
21	60.2 (continues 20)	Nov.	974-77	Weston	Oct. 11, 1790
22	60.2	Nov.	993	P. T. /(Philip Thicknesse)	Nov. 4, 1790
23	60.2	Nov.	1005-06	W.	Nov. 9, 1790
24	60.2	Dec.	1067-68	Reston	Dec. 23, 1790
25	60.2	Dec.	1070-71	J.S.	Nov. 30, 1790

26	60.2	Suppl.	1169-72	Weston	Dec. 23, 1790
	(continues 24)				
27	60.2	Suppl.	1172	Weston	Jan. 3, 1791
28	60.2	Suppl.	1177-78	B.L.A.	Oct. 27, 1790
29	60.2	Suppl.	1197-98	R.W. or /Bardus Ordovicensis	Sept. 22, 1790
30	60.2	Suppl.	1198	R.B.	Nov. 27, 1790
31	61.1	Jan.	8	David /Dalrymple (Lord Hailes)	Jan. 1, 1791
32	61.1	Feb.	138-40	Weston	Feb. 22, 1791
33	61.1	Mar.	224-25	Norfol- /ciensis	Mar. 5, 1791
34	61.1	Mar.	232	D.R.	Mar. 16, 1791
35	61.1	Apr.	300-04	Weston	Apr. 15, 1791

THE LETTERS

1a.

Mr. Urban, *April* 25. [1789]

A Publication has lately appeared, intituled [sic], The Woodmen of Arden. It consists of an ingenious Latin poem by Mr. Morfitt, with two translations of it by Mr. Weston;[1] one literal, in blank verse; the other paraphrastic, and in rhyme. I think highly of Mr. Weston's genius; I know that he has many virtues; and I cannot but be grateful for that partiality to me which his writings have more than once displayed. In the close of a systematic Preface to his translation in rhyme, mentioned above, appears a phantom of imputed perfection, to which he has most inapplicably given *my* name. Mr. Weston is a being whose prejudices are as strong as his talents. In this same Preface, he accuses Pope of having meanly *influenced* his friends to exalt his compositions above their just level, for the purpose of Dryden's, and tearing the laurels from his brow.[2] I believe Pope injured by this accusation; and I am afraid that my acquaintance with Mr. W. and the *hyperbole* of his encomium, should subject *me* to a similar imputation, and induce many to believe that the general assertions of that Preface have my concurrence.

Hence it is that I wish you would allow a place in your Magazine to the ensuing strictures. In combat with the opinions of a man I esteem, to whom I am obliged, they were drawn from me by jealousy, "even to a Roman strictness,"[3] for the poetic glory of the last half-century.

It is probable the length of these observations may render it inconvenient to comprise them in one, or even in two Magazines. Should you divide them, and should Mr. W. reply before their course is finished, I declare that I will *not* be led into new paths of controversy. My business is with the Preface to The Woodmen of Arden.

In the first place, it asserts the Author's opinion, that English Rhyme was brought to the *acme* of *perfection* by Dryden; that, since his time, it has been gradually declining from *good* to *indifferent*, and from *indifferent* to *bad*; and this *bad*, Mr. W. calls the *modern style of versification.* Farther on in the Essay, he avows an ardent desire to see the Pierian spring restored to what he calls Drydenical purity; asserting, that it was corrupted by Pope, and has been poisoned by his successors.[4]

43

In *this*, in every age, since first the light of Poesy dawned, there have been fifty pretenders to its inspirations for one that has been really inspired; but no person in their senses will affirm, that the poetic character of any period takes its colour from the *poetasters* who infest it. Mr. W. cannot be so absurd as to bring *such* of our scribblers into comparison with the illustrious bards of Milton and Dryden's day, and of Pope's and Prior's.

By the Moderns, therefore, Mr. W. must be supposed to mean the *celebrated* poetic writer's [sic] from Pope's decease to the present hour. Let us look at the distinct lustre of the three periods to which he alludes.[5]

The first shone by the light of Milton's genius, of Dryden's, Otway's, Cowley's, Waller's, Davenant's, Butler's, Denham's, Lee's, Lord Roscommon's.

The second, generally called the Augustan age, by that of Pope, Prior, Young, Gay, Swift, Addison, Tickell, Rowe, Congreve, Parnell, Arbuthnot, Steele, Philips, Watts, Lady M. W. Montague.

Ours, by that of Gray, Hayley, Mason, Thomson, Collins, Akenside, the two Wartons, Cowper, Jephson, Goldsmith, Johnson, Beattie, Churchill, Shenstone, Langhorne, Sir William Jones, Pye, Mallet, Owen Cambridge (whose epic satire on Antiquarianism, The Scribleriad,[6] is, perhaps, the best mock-heroic poem in the language except the Dunciad), Sheridan, Lowth, Sarjent, Whalley, Mathias, Jerningham, Whitehead, Horace Walpole, and Cha. Fox whose poetic brilliants, though small, are of the first water), Lloyd, Wesley (author of the noble allegoric poem The Battle of the Sexes),[7] Dyer, Potter, the two Hooles, Hawkins Browne, Somervile, Crabbe, Cawthorne, Home, Crowe, Stevens [Steevens] (author of a fine poem in blank verse called Retirement),[8] Garrick, Murphy, De la Crusca, Cumberland, Greathed, Swift (a spirited satiric poet), Barry, Butt (whose fame has been blighted by too free an use of the Drydenic licences as to versification), the witty, but irreverent, Peter Pindar, the two Cunninghams, the Seven* celebrated Female Poets, Barbauld, More, Williams, Piozzi, Carter, Cowley, Cath. [Charlotte] Smith, the rising poetic lights, Cary and Lister, the unschooled sons of genius, Burns (who is our new Allen Ramsay), Newton, Yearsley, Reid, and the greatest of these wonders, the ill-starred Chatterton, who, had he lived, and his ripe years borne proportionate fruits, must have been the first Poet in the world.

Yours, &c. Anna Seward.

(*To be continued.*)

---

* Fear of offending an amiable correspondent prevents our changing this to Eight. Edit.

1b.

Miss Seward's Strictures on the Preface to the Woodmen of Arden;
(*continued from* [*GM*] p. 292)

If I had not been in some sort addressing him, I should certainly have added the name of Weston to the last*, and (Milton excepted) far the brightest, as well as greatly the most numerous, of the three lists; for Mr. W. has genius to vie with most of his contemporaries, if Prejudice had not chained him to Dryden's car, and persuaded him to take the dirt upon its wheels for studs of jet, placed *purposely* there, as foils to its golden axis [sic].

Have they of this third list collectively "poisoned the Pierian Spring,"[9] either respecting sentiment, imagery, or style? The imputation is injurious, and demands public refutation.

In order to prove Pope's long-confessed refinements to have been real corruptions, Mr. W. asks some ingenious questions concerning the eligibility of keeping down certain parts in poetic composition, upon the painter's system, to give more effect to the brilliant passages.[10] Judgement will readily confess, that the system should be adopted by the sister science; but the manly and graceful plainness of style, such as frequently occurs in *Milton's* poetry, form its *judicious* shades; nor is Pope's by any means destitute of these mellowings; but incongruous metaphor, inconsistent fable, and prating familiarity of expression, instead of softening down, at intervals, the too obtrusive lights of composition, blot, and defile it. With such errors did the *great* Dryden *too often* corrupt the living waters of that Pierian Spring, to which his genius gave him perpetual access.[11]

The Essay in question enumerates what it calls *tinkling* compound epithets amongst the fancied improvements of the Moderns.[12] Tinkling is a most inapplicable adjective; since when, *ill* chosen compound epithets may be stiff, may *grate*, but cannot *tinkle* on the ear. When *well* chosen, their merit is not to the *ear*, but to the *understanding*, by their condensing and energetic power. They are of the Miltonic, not of the Popeian school, and are too seldom used by its disciples.

Our Drydenic enthusiast has certainly convicted Prior and Montague's able criticism upon the Hind and Panther, of one *trivial* mistake, viz. their idea that the words *fated* and *doomed* are exactly synonymous.[13] He calls *that* criticism a wretched abortion; with what justice, let the following quotation from it decide. It is given from memory, and therefore perhaps not verbatim; but the sense is faithful.

45

"Though the fables of the ancients carry a double meaning, the story is one and entire, the characters not broken and changed, but always conformable to the nature of the creatures they introduce. They never tell us that the dog which snapt at a shadow lost his troop of horse; *that* would be unintelligible. It is Dryden's new way of telling a story, to confound the moral and the fable together. How can we conceive a panther reading in a Bible? and what relation has the hind to our Saviour? If you say he means the ancient church, how can we imagine an eating and walking church, feeding on lawns, and ranging in forests? Let it, at least, be *always* a *church*, or always a cloven-footed beast; common sense cannot endure his shifting the scene every line."[14]

Extreme must be the prejudice that can induce a man of genius to deem observations, so indisputably just, the abortive effects of malice. Where the understanding is thus outraged, can it be in melody, sweet as even *Pope's*, to make compensation? and in the Hind and Panther we only find some harmonious and picturesque lines amidst a tedious number of pages, filled with dry, prolix jingles of senseless controversy.

It is curious that Mr. W. should have selected the eight charming verses, which open the Hind and Panther, as specimens of *fine style*,[15] since they are not in *Dryden's* general manner, but exactly in that of *Pope* and his *disciples*, — without one Alexandrine or triplet; with much point and antithesis, and with the sense only once, and that slightly, but very beautifully, overflowing the couplet.

It always appeared to me, that Pope formed his style upon a few of the best passages in Dryden. Mr. W. is very angry with him for separating the dross from the gold.

Pope's numbers seem to have but one fault; viz. the sense, as Mr. W. observes, is too generally confined within the boundary of the couplet;[16] but *that* is surely better than its overflowing too often, as in Dryden's. — My ear dislikes the drag occasioned in the versification of the latter by his placing Alexandrines so frequently in the *middle* of sentences: when harmoniously constructed, they have a majestic effect on *closing* them, even in the heroic measure; but surely the frequent triplets are very botching. I find more *sameness* in Dryden's everlasting Iambics than in that which results from the sense being too seldom allowed to float into the first line of the ensuing couplet for its pause, as in Pope. He uses the spirited accent upon the first syllable in a verse twenty times for once that it occurs in Dryden; and where several objects are to be described in succession, he generally takes the inverted order of the words and the natural one alternately, as in the following passage from a recently published poem of infinite beauty:

46

Pale shoot the stars across the troubled night;
The timid Moon withdraws her conscious light;
Shrill scream the famish'd batts, and shivering owls,
And loud and long the dog of midnight howls. [17]

Another species of superior excellence in Pope's verses over those of Dryden; the former describe in the lively dramatic *present* tense much oftener than the latter. The passage quoted above is in *Pope's* style. Had it run *thus*, it had been in *Dryden's*, and perhaps not in his worst manner:

The stars shot pale across the troubled night,
And the affrighted Moon withdrew her light;
And hungry batts, and owls, and ravens prowl'd,
And, to increase the din, the dog of midnight howl'd.

By this alteration the lines are all Iambics, and have therefore less solemn force of sound.

Mr. Weston complains that Pope is too regularly harmonious. [18] I have selected, out of countless instances, the following passage, in proof that he spared not, occasionally, to use harsh numbers for *picturesque* purposes.

First march the heavy mules, securely slow,
O'er hills, o'er dales, o'er crags, o'er rocks they go;
Jumping high o'er the shrubs of the rough ground,
Rattle the clattering cars, and the shock'd axles bound.
But when arriv'd at Ida's spreading woods,
Fair Ida! water'd with descending floods,
Loud sounds the axe, redoubling strokes on strokes,
On all sides round the forest hurls her oaks;
Headlong, deep echoing, groan the thickets brown,
And rattling [Then rustling], cracking, crashing, thunder down:
                          [*Il.* 8:23.140-49.]

Let us look at a passage in Dryden, whose harshness of numbers is *not* picturesque.

Was there no milder way but the small-pox,
The very filthiness of Pandora's box?
So many spots, like naeves in Venus' soil! [19]
One jewel set off by [with] so *many foil***!
Blisters, with pride swell'd, that [which] through's flesh did sprout,
Like rose-buds stuck i'th' lily skin about.
Each little pimple had a tear in it,
To wail the fault its rising did commit;

47

Which, [Who] rebel-like, with its [their] own lord at strife,
Thus made an insurrection 'gainst his life.
Or were these gems sent to adorn his skin,
The cabinet of a richer soul within?
No comet need foretell his change drew on,
Whose corpse might seem a constellation.   [*UDH* 1:53-66.]

To say nothing of the odiousness of these ideas, or rather conceits, let the passage be viewed as style merely; a specimen of the purity of Dryden's Pierian Spring, which Pope is accused of having corrupted. If it be urged, that this extract is from a juvenile poem of Dryden's, be it remembered that Pope wrote his Pastorals, and the first part of sweet Windsor Forest, two years earlier in life. Thus, at sixteen, did Pope corrupt the Aonian fountain.

His Pastorals.

Thyrsis, the music of the [that] murmuring spring
Is not so mournful as the lays [Strains] you sing;
Nor rivers, winding through the vale [vales] below,
So sweetly warble, or so smoothly flow.
Now sleeping flocks on their soft fleeces lie,
The moon, serene in glory, mounts the sky;
While silent birds forget their tuneful lays,
Sing [Oh sing] of thy Daphne's fate, thy [and] Daphne's praise.
[*Wint.* 1:1-8.]

As an instance that Dryden, in his riper years, was prone to let his style fall below the poetic level where the subject called *aloud* for elevation, observe how the Empress of Heaven is made to open her indignant soliloquy, in his translation of the Aeneid:

Then am I vanquish'd, must I yield, *said she*,
And must the Trojans reign in Italy?
So Fate will have it, and Jove adds his force,
Nor can my power divert their *happy* course.
Could angry Pallas, with revengeful spleen,
The Grecian navy *burn*, and *drown* the *men*,
And cannot I, &c.[20]   [*Ae* 1:56-62.]

Six lines after, Juno says,

The wretch, yet hissing with her father's flame;   [67.]

and thus describes the victim of Minerva's wrath, as Falstaff describes himself reeking from the buck-basket,

Hissing hot, Master Ford, hissing hot.[21]

Now let us compare the style of the two poets, assuming the persons of females, and addressing their lovers, — Helen her Paris, Eloisa her Abelard.

Dryden's Epistle from Helen to Paris.

The crown of Troy is powerful, I confess,
Yet [But] I have reason to think ours no less;
But 'tis your love *moves* me, which made you take
Such pains, and run such hazards for my sake.
I have perceiv'd, though *I dissembled too,*
A thousand things that Love has *made you do*;
Your eager eyes would almost dazzle mine,
In which, wild man, your wanton thoughts would shine.
Sometimes you'd sigh, sometimes disorder'd stand,
And with unusual ardour press my hand.
Contrive, just after me, to take the glass,
Nor would you let the least occasion pass;
When oft I fear'd *I did not mind* alone,
But [and] blushing sat for things which you have done.
Then murmur'd to myself, *"he'll* for my sake
Do any thing," — *I hope 'twas no mistake.*
Oft have I read, within this pleasing grove,
Under my name, [those] charming words, "I love!"
I, frowning, seem'd not to believe your flame,
But now, alas! *am come to write the same.*
For O! your *face* has such peculiar charms,
That who *can hold from* flying to your arms?

                                    [*HP* 1:61-62, 73-90, 93-94.]

This is the style to which Mr. W. seeks to draw us *back* from the *corruptions* of the following.

Eloisa to Abelard.

Thou know'st how guiltless first I met thy flame,
When Love approach'd me under Friendship's name.
My fancy form'd thee of angelic kind,
Some emanation of th' all-beauteous mind;
Those smiling eyes, attempering every ray,
Shone sweetly lambent with celestial day.
From lips like those what precepts fail'd to move?
Too soon they taught me, 'twas no sin to love.

Dim and remote the joys of saints I see,
Nor envy them that heaven I lose for thee.
                                    [2:59-64, 67-68, 71-72.]

A little more from Dryden's Cheapside Miss, married to Menelaus:

Your Trojan wealth, believe me, I despise,
My own poor native land has dearer ties;
I cannot doubt [Nor can I doubt] but, should I follow you,
The sword would soon our fatal crime pursue;
A wrong so great my husband's race [rage] would rouse,
And *my relations would his cause espouse.*
You boast your strength and courage, but alas!
Your words receive small credit from your face.
                                    [*HP* 1: 220-21, 238-43.]

So Helen tells her lover he looks like a sneaking coward, so *ill* does she *express* this compliment to his complexion.
    A little more from Pope's charming Nun:

No weeping orphan saw his father's stores
Our shrines irradiate, or emblaze our floors!
But such plain roofs as Piety could raise,
And only vocal with their Maker's praise.
In these lone walls (their day's eternal bound)
These moss-grown domes, with spiry turrets crown'd,
Where aweful arches make a noon-day night,
And the dim windows shed a solemn light,
Thy eyes diffus'd a reconciling ray,
And gleams of glory brighten'd all the day.
But now no face divine contentment wears,
'Tis all blank sadness and [or] continual tears.
                                    [*ElAb* 2:135-36, 139-48.]

The lines which, in the poem, succeed to the above passage, and form a description of the Paraclete scenery, yield to no poetry as *landscape painting.* Dryden never equaled, and Milton has not excelled, them. The landscape is as *original* as it is solemn and striking, and the sound of the versification breathes the very spirit of elevated melancholy.
                        (*To be concluded in our next.*)

---

* The author of these Strictures is shocked to perceive that she had, through haste, omitted to mention the distinguished names, Lyttleton, Anstey, Mickle, Jekyll, [see Appendix, Part 2] amid her former enumeration of the Poetic Writers in the last half-century. She will probably feel future pain from recollecting several others, whom the incompetence of her memory alone prevented from being named to the honour of the times in which she has lived.

** Bad grammar.

1c.

Miss Seward's Strictures on the Preface to the Woodmen of Arden; (*concluded from* [GM] *p. 391*.

Few, Mr. Urban, that attend to the extracts in your last number, will think Mr. Weston *wise in rejecting* the excuse which Friendship, less blinded by injudicious zeal, alledges for the frequent coarseness of Dryden's ideas, and the frequent bathos of his style, viz. "writing for bread, he had not time to choose and reject his thoughts, to polish and refine his language."[22] But its being known that he never expunged, or even altered, a single passage in the course of those various editions of his Poems that passed under his eye, prove that the pruning knife and the chissel were *not* voluntarily withheld; since it is impossible to conceive that there ever lived a man so notoriously conceited as that, in repeated revision of so many volumes he could see no passage, nor even expression, that he wished to omit or alter. It is therefore plain that Dryden found his wilderness so weedy, that to attempt clearing it would be an Herculean labour, swallowing up that time which he wanted to employ in pressing on with *new* publications, for whose profits his necessities so loudly called. — He trusted to the majestic trees of this wilderness, "laden with blooming gold,"[23] for the preservation of his fame and they *will* preserve it. But he little dreamt that their fruits should so far intoxicate the brain of a brother poet, in future time, as that he should assert the superior beauty of this wilderness on *account* of its weeds, and abuse the majestic parks and lawns of succeeding bards, from which the nettles and switch-grass have been rooted up.

It is also terribly impolitic in Mr. Weston to bring Dryden and Pope in to view *at once*, and then to attack the moral character of the latter, whose imputed crime must be only conjectural; and whose errors are, compared with the mean faults of Dryden, but as a passing cloud of Summer to December's darkness.

Pope did every justice to Dryden's genius; witness one amongst many lines in his praise:

And what Timotheus *was* is Dryden now.   [EOC 1:383.]

51

But in that style in which they both *chiefly* wrote (for Pope was *not* a master of *lyric* composition) he felt his own superiority; not *vainly*, because thousands felt, and still feel it also. He probably wished to see it *asserted*. Why should that wish be deemed proof of a bad heart, even if he did finesse a little to obtain it?

Dryden's writings prove that he was wholly without fixed principles in Religion, Politics, or Criticism; that his Interest was his Legislator, his Guide, and his God. Witness his mean and profane renunciation of the religion in which he had been educated, and had ably defended, for the idolatries he had stigmatised! A Popish King just then mounted on the throne, *who* discerns not the court parasite in the new apostate? Witness his hyperbolic praise of the deceased Cromwell, to please the Republicans, whose downfall he did not then foresee! — and witness his subsequent *abuse* of Cromwell, who being dead when he extolled him, the Poet had no excuse, from any after-conduct of the imputed *angel*, for changing him into a *devil*. Even Mr. W. allows that he formed his critical opinions according to the interest of the hour, callous to all the self-contradictions into which such meanness betrayed him.

How inconceivable is it, that beneath the obtrusive prominence of such faults in Dryden, the writer, who compares the two poets, *can* be severe upon the human frailities of Pope, relieving the necessities of his abusive foe, and watching, with filial tenderness, by the couch of his aged mother!

Mr. W's observation is just upon Dryden's Alexandrine,[24] reprobated by Dr. Johnson, in his Life of that Poet.[25] But to reprobate poetic excellence was Dr. Johnson's *custom*; a thrice dangerous one to the public taste, since it requires unusual strength of mind to escape the pernicious influence of that wit and force of language,

> which can make the *worse* appear
> The *better* reason, to perplex and dash
> True criticism.[26]

The line reprobated by the despot is this:

> And with paternal thunder *vindicates* his throne.[27]
>
> [*HAP* 2:2.537.]

Mr. W. justly defends its dignity of sound.

> And, like another Helen, *fir'd* another Troy,
>
> [*AF* 3:150, 154.]

is upon the *same* construction. But it appears to me that *this* is the only variation from its perfect model that the ear *endures* in the Alexandrine; though Mr. W. affirms that the pause may be placed after *any* of its syllables, without injury to the harmony.[28]

The next line, quoted in *proof* of that assertion, is to *my* ear a doleful drag, little resembling a *verse*:

> By many follow'd, lov'd by most, admir'd by all.

There are several of *kindred* imperfection in Guiscard and Sigismunda; for instance:

> *Like Liberty, indulg'd with choice of good and [or] ill, and*
> *A pomp, prepar'd to grace the present be design'd.*   [*SG* 4:509, 608.]

Those lines, if read with *proper* emphasis, are *not* verse, though they may *scan* as such, since the *sense* allows no pause after the words *indulg'd* and *grace*.

Mr. W. asserts the poetic right of intermixing, at pleasure, lines of fourteen syllables into the common heroic couplet.[29] The first line quoted from Dryden, to illustrate the claim,

> But Maurus sweeps whole parishes, and peoples every grave,
>   [*TJD* 4:83.]

has such strength of thought and imagery, that they atone for *any* liberty, however generally unjustifiable, that may be taken with the numbers; but the *next* citation,

> The tedious [nauseous] qualms of nine [ten] long months,
> and travail, to require   [*VP4* 4:75.],

possessing nothing stiking or poetic in the *thought*, it cannot surely be in the mere echo of its sound to its sense to recompense the bad effect of putting a line and three quarters, of eight feet measure, into *one*, and then drawing it through the texture of the couplet numbers, like a hoop, five yards wide, stuck across the limbs of an elegant maid of honour!

This *last* Drydenic licence sounds to me like ludicrous ballads, part of which are sung, and then a line *said*.

> Captain Colvert's gone to sea, heigh boys! ho boys!
> Captain Colvert's gone to sea, O!
> Captain Colvert's gone to sea, with all his company,
> In the great Benjamin, ho!

> Now you shall hear how he was cast upon an uninhabited
> island, and married the governor's daughter.
> Captain Colvert's gone to sea, &c.[30]

Mr. W. gives to Pope's patrons amongst the nobility the title of *wou'd be Maecenases*.[31] The phrase is invidious; and his poetic brethren of this day are not much obliged to him for thus discouraging poetic patronage; for assisting to spread that Gothic mantle over the Muses which the dark huge hands of the envious Colossus first unfurl'd in the Lives of the Poets. Either Horace has had more injustice from his translators, Cowley, Dryden, and even Milton of the number, than ever poet met, or those whom Mr. W. calls the wou'd-be Maecenases patronised a *greater* poet than *Horace*.

Mr. Weston writes in this Preface as if the excellence or worthlessness of a poem depended wholly upon the construction of its *measure*; and as if the couplet was the only order of rhyme. He seems to forget that the lyric, with its countless varieties, and almost unlimited privileges, affords ample field for his alexandrines and triplets, whose frequent intermixture suits not the chastity of the heroic couplet; though it appears to me that it is by no means an advantage to make the sense so generally end with the second line, as in the otherwise *perfect* style of Pope's versification.

After all, it is a small part of the intrinsic excellence of poetry that the elegant style of Pope, or the slovenly one of Dryden, can give or take away. A poem has little merit if it does not remain fine poetry after having been taken out of *all* measure. Where there is loftiness of thought, ingenuity of allusion, and strength of imagery, to stand *that* test, true lovers of the art allow an author to do almost what he pleases with the numbers, provided he does not insist upon their preference of the slovenly to the polished ones, readily promising that such a work shall be dear to them in *any* dress. They will by no means wish that *every* part should blaze; but would *chuse* that there should be "interstices of black velvet between the gems;"[32] desiring, however, to be excused from *applauding* the custom of *Dryden's* Muse, to put on "soiled linen with her diamonds."[33]

Several of Mr. W's poetic friends, as well as himself, are surprised that any person can prefer his *close* translation of Mr. Morfitt's fine Latin poem to his more ingenious *paraphrastic* one. He and they, must however *expect* that preference from those who agree with him in thinking that Pope has degenerated from Dryden in the beauty and purity of style. My friend will find many who, because the latter-named poet lived a degree more remote from the present day than the former, will decree the palm of pre-eminence to *him*; but whatever author shall be rash enough to resume the slip-shod licences of Dryden, *see* if they will applaud the result. Not they; even though it should be adorned with all the riches of allusion and imagery which glow through the writings of Mr. Weston. His Miltonic Sonnets appear to me models of perfection in that arduous order of poetic composition.   Anna Seward.

2.

Mr. Urban,   *May* 30. [1789]
    I was much concerned to observe, [*GM*] vol. LVIII, p. 1060, that Mr. Weston, in his very just and reasonable appeal to the publick on the premature, incorrect, and clandestine appearance of his poetry, in the conclusion should apply such an harsh epithet as "execrable"[34] to Mr. Pope, that favourite of the Muses, whose harmonious numbers, elegant sensibility, condensation of good sense, poignant wit, delicacy and taste, have, and will continue to charm thousands, as long as our language has existence. I doubt not Mr. Welsted had his excellencies. I am willing to allow him every merit, as Poet and a Man, that Mr. Weston attributes to him, and that he has been too severely satirised by Mr. Pope;[35] and in abatement of Mr. Pope's character, will allow he might have a spark of envy in his composition; that he might be too irritable, too peevish, that he would

Bear, like the Turk, no brother near the throne. [*EpArb.* 4:198.]

Yet who does not know that exalted genius and first-rate talents generally have too high a sense of their own superiority, and are too apt to bear hard on those a few degrees below them, and, from a fear or envy of their rising merit, will depreciate that they really possess? Undoubtedly it is wrong; and in the particular instance under consideration, Mr. Pope might and did diffuse his satiric wit with unmerited acrimony: yet, though I blame, I cannot execrate him for it. My Dictionary says the word means *hateful, destestable, abominable, very wicked, odious,* or *impious*; surely Mr. P. cannot deserve all these; if he did, he might as justly be said to deserve a halter. I hope Mr. Weston, on a retrospect, will regret that the word escaped him; and I wish he may think a gentler term more just and applicable in the comparison of Pope and Welsted.

                                                              Yours, &c. M. F.

3.
Mr. Urban,   *Solihull, July* 20. [1789]
[Weston postpones his reply because of illness and promises to reply both to Miss Seward and M.F.]

... and I will then endeavour to prove, that my fair and most respectable opponent has been *for once* mistaken — that the Critical Reviewers deserve a scourge — and that Pope, however the assertion may shock M. F., really *did* deserve — What He Mentions.

Yours, &c. Joseph Weston.

4.
Mr. Urban,   *Solihull, Aug.* 23. [1789]
When I published the Woodmen of Arden I was perfectly aware that, unless the Poem should steal quietly along into the Vale of Oblivion, the Preface would furnish an ample subject for animadversion. My dislike to Pope's Versification, my detestation of his Principles, and the indignation which I felt that so many wise and so many worthy persons should have become the Dupes of an *Imposter*, hurried on my pen with a degree of vehemence that set Fear at defiance. But, though, on cool reflection, I entertained some doubts of the prudence of my conduct, I had none of the justice of my cause; and, reposing with confidence on arguments which I conceived would not easily be confuted, I felt little apprehension that any Antagonist would start up in a *very* formidable shape.

But I was too blindly secure. An Antagonist *has* started up in a most formidable shape *indeed* — viz. that of a Friend; armed too with weapons of the most formidable kind — Candour, Politeness, and Generosity: and, to form a regular climax of distress, that candid, polite, and generous Friend, is a Woman; a beautiful, accomplished, and amiable Woman! Can a more perplexing dilemma be imagined than that which presents itself? Could a more disagreeable predicament be invented than that in which I stand?

I am attacked by one of the finest Writers of the Age, with the united force of brilliant Wit, magnificent Metaphor, and critical Acumen. What must I do? Must I defend myself, or must I fly the field? Disgrace awaits me on either hand. *If* I defend myself, who can tell that, in the warmth of argument, a *strenuous* defence may not undesignedly be converted into an Attack? And what a pitiful figure does one of Homer's Heroes make while wounding a Goddess! If, to avoid this danger, I give ground to my fair Antagonist, will the World give me credit for my Magnanimity? No. — Will my fair Antagonist herself give me credit for it? No. — To decline the proffered combat would, in her eyes, as well as in those of the publick, betray a consciousness of a weak cause; and, perhaps, seem an insolent affectation of superiority: and both her sense and her spirit would, I am sure, reject with scorn the idea of being indebted to my forbearance or compassion. . . . Nor do I know *which* mode of conduct I might ultimately have adopted, had not a new opponent rushed into the field, to offer his assistance to one who is herself An Host!

> "Non tali auxilio nec defensoribus istis
> "Seward eget."[36]

I feel so grateful for this strange Knight's unexpected interference (which has so considerably lessened my embarrassment), that I am not much disposed to enquire if I am obliged, by the laws of chivalry, to accept the challenge of one who has slept for six months over the supposed provocation: nor will I urge the still stronger objection that this unknown Adversary comes in disguise, and refuses to declare his name and rank in arms. Though, from the gentle and courteous terms in which his defiance is couched, I believe him to be of no vulgar degree, I cannot but think the behaviour of my first Opponent infinitely more intitled to respect, who, with the grace and dignity of a Thalestris, while with one hand she shakes her glittering spear, with the other lifts her beaver, and discovers a countenance that melts down all opposition, and eyes that dim the radiance of the gems that spangle-o'er her burnished helmet.

I may now, Mr. Urban, content myself with parrying some of this *literary Amazon's* most dangerous thrusts, and secure a not inglorious retreat, to try my strength upon her Auxiliary.

As the Strictures on my Preface are extended to *three* Numbers, I shall extend my observations on them to three Numbers also; a method which, in the present state of my health, I shall find peculiarly convenient. Letter the first, in your Magazine for April, will give me no great trouble, as there is very little business done in *that*, except summoning the Court, opening the Commission, and calling over the names of the Jurymen; to every one of which I object, however, from motives of sound policy. Though they may be all *good men and true*, I claim the privilege (allowed in the court of Apollo at least) of *challenging* every mother's son of them, lest those, whom as interested persons I reject, should deafen the Court with the clamours of their resentment. — No. — If I *must* be put upon my defence, e'en let my fair *Accuser*, whom, as Mr. Hayley has acknowledged her to be "the leader of the female Train,"[37] I will also allow to be my *Judge*, make up her Seven female Poets a Dozen, and let me be tried by Them! I shall then stand a chance of a favourable Verdict, as I can conscientiously affirm, that *their* share of the Censure which I have bestowed on the Moderns will be very trifling indeed.

Two Mistakes occur in Miss Seward's Exordium. I have neither imputed to Her a single Perfection which she does not possess, nor have I accused Pope "of having meanly *influenced* his friends to exalt his Compositions above their just Level, for the purpose of lowering Dryden's and tearing the Laurels from his his Brow."[38]

All who have the Honour and Happiness of Miss Seward's Acquaintance, must own that I might have considerably enlarged the Catalogue of her Virtues without the least violation of Truth; and, on a reference to my preface (p.14), it will be found that I only glanced at "the insidious arts which Pope *suffered* his Friends to practise, in order to undermine the Reputation of the deceased Poet, and to asperse the Characters of his living Supporters."[39] But I will not insist on the Distinction; for, although the difference between *influencing* and *permitting* may appear at first sight material, I will frankly confess, that *I* should be inclined to consider the person who commits a crime, and the person who, with the power to *prevent* it, suffers that crime to committed, for the sake of his own advantage, as nearly upon an equality.

I shall reserve to a more proper place[40] what I have further to say on this point, and proceed to remark, that Miss Seward is perfectly right when she supposes, that by the Moderns I mean the *celebrated* Poetic Writers from Pope's decease to the present hour — (indeed I could not possibly mean the *Poetasters*): and a most tremendous Phalanx, in Battle-array, has she brought against poor me!

The plan which I have proposed to myself will not permit me to reply *now* to the question which she so triumphantly asks, in the beginning of her *second* letter; but I most sincerely admire her spirit and good-sense in restoring to that rank, from which Dr. Johnson so unjustly degraded him, Sir William Davenant,[41] who, in spite of the illiberal ridicule of the profligate Villiers,[42] and in spite of the instances of false Taste which may be found in his Writings, had yet Spirit, Sense, Genius, and Morality, sufficient to secure for him a very high place among the Bards of Charles's days.

Had our Arch-critic read, or at least recollected, a Stanza with which I shall conclude this Address, its superlative merit (doubly endeared to Him by the nature of the Subject) would have pleaded hard for the unfortunate Author's admission into the Poetic Corps, even though, to make room for him, Johnson should have been obliged to thrust from their unmerited situations *Duke, Stepney, Yalden, Pomfret*,[43] and many more, whom the good Doctor seems to have lugged out of Oblivion, for the mere Purpose of "exalting the humble, and bringing the mighty low!"[44]

> *O, harmless* Death, whom still the Valiant *brave,*
> The Wise *expect,* the Sorrowful *invite,*
> And all the Good *embrace,* who know the Grave
> A *short, dark* passage to Eternal Light!
> *The Dying Reply to the Philosopher.*[45]

Yours, &c. Joseph Weston.

5.

Mr. Urban, *Aug. 5.* [1789]

The publick could not but be obliged to Mr. Weston, if he had no other merit than that of having called forth those animated and ingenious strictures which have lately graced the pages of your Miscellany. Yet, much as I admire the good sense and taste of the fair writer, I cannot help thinking that she has overstepped the limits of justice, and that, in endeavouring to vindicate Pope and the moderns from some undeserved accusations, she has been too hard upon Dryden, and totally unfair in her estimation of the poets of preceding times. Is not the lustre of Pope's period considerably diminished by the absence of the names of Akenside, Hammond, Collins, Thomson, Mallet, Lyttelton, A. Philips, Welsted, Allen Ramsay, Glover, Broome, Shenstone, Somervile, Pomfret, Hughes, Garth, the Duke of Buckingham, and Dennis?[46] The list of poetic writers in Milton's age might be swelled to an equal amount, if all those who were admired during their lives were admitted. But it must be more than common excellence which can insure a reputation of an hundred years; and probably in that space many of those luminaries, which contribute to the splendour of the present day, will be extinguished and forgotten. That Dryden purposely kept down certain parts of his writings, in order to serve as foils to the rest, is an assertion in which Mr. W. will not, perhaps, find a single advocate; as the prematurity in which pecuniary circumstances compelled him to hurry his publications into the world is known and lamented by every one. Had he polished with the minute skill and diligence of Pope, he would have been without an equal in his line. But since the unfortunate state of his affairs denied him leisure to do so, let us throw a veil over his blemishes, and exhibit with conscious pride the numerous beauties of our noble countryman.

59

Instead of this, Miss S. has extracted the most dark and blotted passages, which are contrasted with the most splendid and graceful lines of his rival. What would she say if a critic, as a specimen of Shakespeare's genius, should produce some of that vile ribaldry which is so plentifully interspersed in the works of our immortal bard? Permit me to shew how Dryden could sometimes write. In his Epistle to Sir Godfrey Kneller are these lines:

> "More cannot be by mortal art exprest,
> But venerable Age shall add the rest;
> For Time shall with his ready pencil stand,
> Retouch your figures with his rip'ning hand,
> Mellow your colours, and imbrown the teint,
> Add ev'ry grace which time alone can grant,
> To future ages shall your fame convey,
> And give more beauties than he takes away."   [1:174-81.]

A description of a storm:

> "The cries of men are mix'd with rattling shrouds.
> Seas dash on seas and clouds encounter clouds;
> At once from East to West, from pole to pole,
> The forky lightnings flash the roaring thunders roll."
>
> [CA 4:121-24.]

Again:

> "No star appears to lend his friendly light,
> Darkness and tempest make a double night;
> But flashing fires disclose the deep by turns,
> And while the lightnings blaze, the water burns."
>
> [CA 4:157-60.]

Nothing can go beyond the following passage in his translation from the Metamorphoses. — The House of Sleep:

> "An arm of Lethe, with a gentle flow,
> Arising upwards from the rock below,
> The palace moats, and o'er the pebbles creeps,
> And with soft murmurs calls the coming sleeps;
> Around its entry nodding poppies grow,
> And all cool simples that sweet rest bestow,
> Night from the plants their sleepy virtue drains
> And passing sheds it on the silent plains."   [CA 4:282-89.]

We cannot wonder at any enthusiasm offered up to the author of the foregoing lines. But, as a friend to the Muses, I regret that Mr. W. should carry his admiration of Dryden so far, as even studiously to imitate his defects. He will find his account, if he has the resolution to make a sacrifice of his own judgement to the public taste, since private prejudice should always give way, in such matters, to universal and established opinion. With pleasure I seize this opportunity of adding my vote to Miss Seward's with respect to Mr. W's Sonnets, which are extremely elegant and highly finished.   M[arcellu]s [Henry Francis Cary]

6.

Mr. Urban,   *Sept.* 8. [1789]
    Mr. Weston, in his answer to Miss Seward, [*GM*] p. 680,[47] is pleased to take umbrage at my presuming to think his *execration* of Mr. Pope harsh and unjustifiable.

["M.F." objects to Weston's calling him a "strange knight" and unknown adversary." He explains the delay in his answering Weston's attack on Pope: "Mr. Urban can inform him that my letter was transmitted at least four months before its insertion."]
    Does Mr. W. suppose it enhances his magnanimity by insulting over the ashes of the venerable dead, and execrating the man who has almost universally been esteemed in the foremost rank of poets, and among the best of men? Would Mr. W. have adventured on the sentence had the admired Pope been living? If so, his hardihood might have excited our astonishment, though I question whether his prudence would have acquired our applause.
    Mr. W. is perfectly right in saying I am "unknown, and in disguise."[48] I acknowledge myself a son of obscurity, "a fellow whom nobody knows;"[49] but in this, as well as in my estimation of Mr. Pope, I plead a majority on my side; I believe more than two-thirds of Mr. Urban's correspondents make use of initials or anonymous signatures. But this is nothing to the matter in hand. What does it avail to the justice of the cause who or what I am? The whole dispute between us is, whether Mr. Pope can be justly deemed Execrable or not, I hold the latter; Mr. W. has pledged himself to prove the former: and, if I mistake not, a very tough piece of work he will have of it. When he has brought forth his "strong reasons," his valid evidences, and laid them before us with those shining talents he is confessedly master of, if they are satisfactory, I shall retain to myself a liberty of yielding to superior evidence, changing my opinion, and becoming his convert; until which time I hope he will let

61

me quietly enjoy my present sentiments, as I have no intentions of occupying Mr. Urban's valuable columns or troubling him or the publick on this subject again. Thus far I thought necessary in my own vindication.   Yours, &c. M. F.

7.

Mr. Urban,   *Lichfield, Sept.* 15. [1789]

You will permit a few comments on the letters in your last number, from my polite antagonists, concerning the subject of Dryden and Pope. Mr. Weston imputes to the latter the meanness of at least *suffering* those preferences of himself to Dryden to get abroad, which appeared so frequently in the public prints during his life-time.

Reflecting one instant *coolly* on the subject, he must have the generosity to withdraw this charge. I have avowed my opinion, that the two writers possessed great and equal genius, and that Pope became, upon the whole, much the finest poet, from that superior taste and judgement which banished those prosing redundancies, those disgusting images, those low expressions, which so often sully and debase the writings of Dryden. Can Mr. W. suppose, were Pope alive, I should have been indelicate enough to consult him before I published my vindication of his character and of his claims? How very improbable that he had power to prevent the appearance of *similar* assertions!

When prejudice and personal enmity peruse Mr. Weston's hyperbolic praise of me, they may, with equal justice, declaim, as he does against Pope, upon the meanness and vanity of my *suffering* its appearance. They will ungenerously conceal their consciousness that it was probably out of my power to suppress what it is certain I never saw till I saw it in print. Knowing *that* truth, he would be shocked at *their* injustice. I hope, therefore, that he will awaken to a sense of his *own*.

In reply to the observation of your ingenious correspondent M — — s [*GM*] p. 682,[50] that the lustre of Pope's period is diminished by the absence of the names of Akenside, Hammond, Collins, Shenstone, with some others of considerable celebrity, I alledge, that the *personal* existence of those writers during that of Pope is of no consequence. He heard Dryden converse in a coffee-room when he was twelve years old, and boasted of the circumstance through life with generous pleasure; but a poet cannot be said to exist till his writings become known. Akenside died so lately as the year 1770, aged forty-nine. His great work, The Pleasures of Imagination, was not published till forty-four, in which year Pope died. Akenside's poetic lustre cannot, therefore, be said to gild the period in which the Bard of Twickenham flourished; it descended upon the *later* times, where the poets are placed whom we mention to the honour of our *own* day. Collins also was not heard of in Pope's life-time. His Odes, descriptive and moral, were first published in the year forty-six, and it was many years before they had either sale or fame. The blindness of the age to their *now* celebrated excellence cost their unfortunate author his reason and his life. His glory, so long eclipsed, first shone on the aera in which I placed the *last*, and by no means the least, powerful division of the bards. The same plea justifies the placing of Shenstone, Hammond, Somervile, Mallet,[51] &c. in the last set, namely, their celebrity not being risen in the meridian of Pope, in the reigns of Anne and George the First, in the age that is styled *Augustan.* Allen Ramsay and the Duke of Buckingham[52] were omitted through forgetfulness in the second list; and in the third, from the same cause, Lyttelton, Ansty, Mickle, Jekyl[l], Polwhele, and our present Tickell.[53] If the poetasters Pomfret and Dennis[54] ought to have been found in the *second* enumeration, there are an *army* of better writers not mentioned in the *third*. I did not chuse to bring forward, for the honour of Pope's period, any of the heroes of his inimitable Dunciad. On examination, I find Thomson ought to have graced the second instead of the third galaxy.[55]

I cannot think with M — — s, that only very superior poets survive their century. On the contrary, it has always seemed to me that antiquity induces the generality of readers to set a double value on every beauty, and to pass over defects with indulgence. Had Dryden's con-temporaries, Denham, Lee, Roscommon, and even Waller, whose names have outlived the centennial limits; had they lived and produced their poems *now*, I do not believe they would have many admirers. Denham's verses are in general heavy, laboured, inharmonious; and Waller's have more courtly wit than poetic fire. In the second division, Parnell, Gay, Addison, Watts, and the two Philips, soar not to the highest eminences of the Aonian mountain; yet each of them have written some things in verse that will probably preserve the honour of their memories so long as our language shall remain. Amongst the least celebrated of the third list, there are few who have not written as well as those second-rate bards of the preceding periods.

Suffer me to assure M — — s, that I produced some of the many bald passages from Dryden, not to lower his name on the ground of possessing a genius creative, rich, and luxuriant, but merely to confute an assertion which, if believed *just*, might tempt our young writers into a coarse and weedy style, Viz. that Dryden's gross defects are happy negligences, voluntarily adopted for the Judicious repose of composition, and in themselves preferable to the chaste, graceful, and polished numbers of Pope.

M — — s says, I have selected the most dark and blotted passages of the elder bard, contrasting them with the most splendid ones of his rival. That was by no means my design; but I thought it fair to make the first selection from the earliest compositions of each; and the Pastorals of Pope, from which the first quotation was made, are the least esteemed of any thing he wrote.

If from Pope's Homer lines can be produced mean and wretched as those which Dryden has, in his Aeneid, put into the mouth of the Empress of Heaven,[56] and if it cannot be proved that such vulgar language occurs on almost every page in Dryden, I will give up the point in contest; which, on my part, goes no farther than to assert, that the poetic writers of *this* day have done honour to their art, by avoiding the botching vulgarities of Dryden's style, and emulating the polished graces of his successor.

It was surely fair to place in one point of view the enamoured epistle by Dryden from Ovid, and that by Pope from Eloisa's Letters to Abelard. All who have sense and taste enough to *attend* to the subject, know that *both* these poets translated upon the only plan which makes translations worth any thing, Viz. to abandon every idea of closeness, and to interweave any new sentiment or imagery that occurs, if it can add grace or spirit to the theme. It is thus that translations justly procure for those who give them the honours of original composition. The most beautiful of Dryden's poetry, in the heroic couplet, is from Ovid, Chaucer, and Boccace. In the epistles from Helen, and Eloisa, their respective translators took similar subjects; and if it is fair to compare the Odes on the Power of Music, for the purpose of decreeing the *lyric* palm to Dryden, it is equally fair to compare the two love epistles, where Pope's superiority over his rival in the *heroic* measure is even more distinguished.

Neither did I, in that comparison, extract the *most* splendid lines from the Eloisa. Those in which she describes herself and Abelard in the hour of her profession; those where she presents herself officiating as priestess amidst the solemnities of the mass; the Paraclete scenerey; the impersonization of Melancholy sitting amongst the twilight groves, dusky caverns, long-sounding ailes, and intermingled tombs of the monastery, and breathing over them a gloom, which shades the flowers, and darkens the umbrage; all those are passages of great poetic superiority to those I quoted from that poem in contrast to the vapid effusions of Helen's ideas from the pen of Dryden. Scarce any traces of the picturesque beauties can be found in the original letters between Abelard and Eloisa; they are the rich creations of an imagination, which, setting style apart, I have not seen transcended by Dryden.

M — — s has quoted some extremely beautiful passages from that confessedly great poet. We often find them interspersed in his writings; but we also find them surrounded and disgraced by verses below mediocrity. The following lines, from Pope to Jervas, are not less excellent that those which M — — s has given us from Dryden's Epistle to Kneller. Speaking of the beautiful women whose pictures had been drawn by Jervas, the Poet says,

> "O! lasting as those colours may they shine,
> Free as thy stroke, and faultless as thy line;
> New graces hourly, [yearly] like thy works, display,
> Soft without weakness, without glaring gay;
> Led by some rule that guides, but not constrains,
> And finish'd more thro' *happiness* than *pains.*
> The kindred arts shall in their praise conspire,
> One dip the pencil, and one string the lyre." [*Ep.J* 6:63-70.]

The ensuing verses, describing seastorms, by Pope, have an equal right to our admiration with those quoted in the last Magazine from Dryden. Both are *free* translations; Dryden's from Ovid, Pope's from Homer.

> "He spoke, and high the forky trident hurl'd,
> Rolls clouds on clouds, and wakes [stirs] the watry world;
> At once the face of sea and sky [earth and sea] deforms,
> Swells all the winds, and rouses all the storms;
> [*Od.* 9:5.375-78.]
> Wide o'er the waste the rage tempestuous sweeps,
> And Night rush'd headlong on the shaded deeps.
> [*Od.* 9.77-78.]
> With what a cloud the brows of Heaven are crown'd!
> [*Od.* 9:78.306.]
> What raging winds, what roaring waters round!
> [*Od.* 9:5.389-90.]
> Now here, now there, the giddy ships are borne,
> [*Od.* 9:79.306.]
> And all the whirling [rattling] shrouds in fragments torn;
> [*Od.* 9:80.306.]
> For, [While] by the howling tempest, rent in twain,
> Flew sail and sail-yards rattling o'er the main."
> [*Od.*9:407-08.]

Dryden's House of Sleep, from the Ceyx and Alcyone of Ovid, is exquisite versification; but, in *that* passage, *all* the imagery and invention is Ovid's. As allegoric painting, Pope's portrait of Dulness, where all the features are *original*, has equal happiness of invention, equal strength of colouring. How often, in the great work from whence it is quoted, do we find the most beautiful flowers of fancy entwined around the rod of satire!

> "Dulness o'er all possess'd her ancient right,
> Daughter of Chaos, and eternal Night;
> Fate, in their dotage, this fair idiot gave,
> Gross as her sire, and as her mother grave;
> Laborious, heavy, busy, bold, and blind,
> She rules in native anarchy the mind.
> Her ample presence fills up all the space,
> A veil of fogs dilates her aweful face."
> [*Dun*B 5:1.11-16 and 261-62.]

A *local* description, what can be more charming than the following lines from the same poem?

> "Lo! where Maeotis sleeps, and scarcely [hardly] flows,
> The freezing Tanais through a waste of snows,
> The North by myriads pours her might sons,
> Great nurse of Goths, of Alans, and of Huns.
> See, where the morning gilds the palmy shore,
> The soil that arts and infant letters bore,
> His conquering tribes th' Arabian prophet draws,
> And saving Ignorance inthrones by laws."
> [*Dun*B 5:3,87-90 and 95-99.]

We may apply to the above extracts from Pope what M——s says after his quotations from Dryden; "we cannot wonder at any enthusiasm offered up to their author."[57]   Yours, &c. Anna Seward.

8a. [continues Letter 4]
Mr. Urban,   *Solihull, Oct.* 26. [1789]
   [Weston says he will interrupt his reply to Miss Seward to reply to "M.F." He defends the terms "strange knight" and "unknown adversary" and says he "did *not* 'take umbrage' (Letter 6) at my execration of Mr. Pope being deemed by M. F. harsh and unjustifiable."]
   I do *not* "insult over the ashes of the *venerable* dead."[58] The man whom, had he been living, I should have regarded with horror, I cannot allow

to have become venerable by ceasing to exist. His *works* exist; and many whose abilities have challenged admiration, and many whose virtues have excited esteem, are consigned to contempt and infamy as long as those works endure. Shall I be deterred by the foolish adage of *"De mortuis nil nisi* Bonum"[59] from entering my protest against such injustice? Shall an assertion, that "Pope has almost universally been esteemed in the foremost rank of poets, and among the best of men,"[60] strike me with such awe, that, though I *can* prove both claims to be unjust, I must not *dare* to do it, lest I should find the Universe in arms against me? Whatever may be the risk, however, I shall do it. *Fiat Justitia, ruat Coelum!*[61]

Shall this Cromwell, who has injured that poetical constitution which he pretended to amend, trampled on the rights of those fellow-citizens whom he ought to have loved and protected, and, by dint of the most hypocritical pretences to piety and morality, imposed on the understandings, and seduced the affections of the rich and the powerful, making them his stepping-stones to the highest seat in the realms of Parnassus; shall this Usurper, I say, who, having thus wickedly gained the throne, vilified the abilities, and assassinated the reputations of those whose claim to it might interfere with his own, and gibbeted all their adherents and abettors, rest undisturbed in the dust? Can the office of tearing him from his grave, that he may be *exalted* for an example to all succeeding tyrants, though disagreeable, be deemed sacrilegious? Is it not even meritorious? Seeming cruelty to the dead is real humanity to the living. — — Who, endued with poetic genius and classical erudition, though, perhaps, not blest with sufficient application, or sufficient leisure, to produce works of an elaborate or an exalted kind, will venture to amuse the world with the light and elegant effusions of Taste and Sensibility, through the medium of your very respectable Miscellany, if some Leviathan of literature, suspecting that the young fry may, some time or other, prove rivals, is at hand, with his enormous jaws distended, to swallow them at a gulp?

Joseph Weston.

---

‡ We must apologize to our readers for this letter's breaking off abruptly. — Mr. W. will know that we were so closely urged in respect of time, that it is not without difficulty we have made room for so much of it. Edit.

8b.

Continuation of Mr. Weston's *Vindication of himself (from [GM]* p.876.)

M. F. exultingly asks, if "I would have adventured on the sentence had the admired Pope been living?" — I certainly would; and M. F. *might* have stared with "astonishment at my Hardihood" and "Imprudence."[62] I might perchance, Mr. Urban, have been rewarded with a place in the Temple of Dulness; and would then have consoled myself for present Disgrace, by the Consciousness of Rectitude, and the Hope that some future Writer might be as just and as generous to Me, as the Conductor of your Magazine has been to the injured and insulted Welsted: for which I *once more* thank him. Were it necessary, I could evince the Sincerity of my Thankfulness, by producing a Poem,[63] written more than a Dozen Years since, 300 Lines of which are appropriated to the honest purpose of rescuing from unmerited Obloquy not only Welsted, but also many other Heroes of the inimitable Dunciad. That Dunciad, upon whose rotten, pestilential Carcase, even the embalming Art of the admirable Seward is exercised in vain! — Inimitable? — Ay, that it is; and so, I believe, will long remain! — Inimitable in its Wit — inimitable in its Malevolence! — But let it rest for the present! I shall pay it another Visit, as soon as I have fulfilled my Engagement with Respect to my Preface to the Woodmen of Arden; from which no more Interruptions from M. F. nor from any one else shall divert me.

When I have dispatched that essential business, I shall endeavour to convince M. F. that he is *again* mistaken; for I shall assuredly find no "*very* tough piece of work" in proving Mr. Pope to be — what no *honest* man Can be. — Nor shall I derive any Assistance from those "shining Talents," of which M. F. obligingly supposes me possessed. I shall state a plain Fact, in plain Language. — My Reasons, it is true, *will* be "strong;" and my Evidence *will* be "valid:" — *such* Reasons and *such* Evidence as M. F. will scarcely controvert; since the single Witness whom I shall produce on the Occasion will be — Pope *himself*! — a Witness who will settle the affair much more effectually than the train of Lords and Commons united could have done, whom he has so ostentatiously called to his Character; and who, it seems, esteemed him "to be in the foremost Rank of Poets, and among the best of Men."

If, in my Journey through Life, I have met with Monsters of *Selfishness, Inhumanity, Hypocrisy,* and *Ingratitude* (and God knows that such monsters I *have* met with!), who, with not the tenth part of Mr. Pope's Cunning, have yet had the Address to impose themselves on very good, nay, very wise Persons, for Models of the opposite Virtues — can I wonder that so great a Master of the Art of Dissimulation contrived to blind those whom the lustre of his Talents had already dazzled?

* * * *

Joseph Weston.†

———

† Mr. W.'s Second Letter next month.

———

8c.

Mr. Urban,   *Solihull, Nov. 23.* [1789]

Unwilling as I am (for Reasons sufficiently obvious) to quote my own Authority, I know not how I can contrive to render my Defence of the Preface to the Woodmen of Arden intelligible to such of your Readers as may entertain no great Fondness for turning backward and forward very many Pages of your Publication, unless I request Admission for some copious Extracts from the Work itself.

Loathing every Species of Affectation, I will not insult your Understanding, by making any long Apology for the Room which they will take up in your valuable Miscellany; since, however erroneous the Opinions contained in the Essay may be thought, however feeble my Justification of them may prove, the Subject, at least, can never be deemed uninteresting to a large Proportion of your Readers, which has had the painful Distinction of arresting the Attention, and of calling forth the critical powers of a Correspondent, whose occasional Contributions so beautifully irradiate the Gentleman's Magazine!

But, left the Liberty which I claim should be construed Licentiousness, I intend to select *only* such Passages as have been the immediate Cause of drawing down upon me Miss Seward's Animadversions; nor shall I select *all* those: conscious that the Parts which are absolutely *necessary* to be adduced will occupy more of your Columns than you can conveniently spare, overwhelmed as you evidently are by such a Multiplicity of Communications. — Give me Leave to suggest, by Way of reconciling you, in some Measure, to the uncommon Length of the Quotations of which I am soliciting the Insertion, that (containing in themselves, as I hope they do, an almost complete Apology) they will materially lessen my present Labour; and, perhaps, engross no larger Portion of your Paper than those Observations probably would, which I must be *obliged* to make, if I should be refused this more summary, and, of course, more eligible Mode of Vindication.

Without further Preamble, then, I proceed to the Essay which is prefixed to *that* Translation of Mr. Morfitt's admirable Latin Poem, which I profess to be *attempted* in the Manner of Dryden.

"To neglect the *modern* Style of Versification — to overlook even that which Pope introduced — and, professedly, to copy from the old fashioned Model of Dryden — will excite some Degree of Surprize among those who take for granted that Poetic Diction has, since his Time, received considerable *Improvement*. — But, to confess the Truth, I cannot help thinking that English Rhyme was brought by that wonderful Man to the *Acme* of Perfection; and that it has been, for many Years, gradually declining from Good to *indifferent* — and from *indifferent* to Bad.

"I am not unaware that a Sentiment so unfavourable to *most* of my contemporaries, and so opposite to Prejudices long received and obstinately retained, will, probably, be considered as the rash and romantic Assertion of a vain and presumptuous Innovator, and be treated with all the Severity usually exercised against Notions which are looked upon as heterodox. — But such Severity would be flagrant Injustice. — The Opinion which I have expressed is neither dictated by Vanity, nor prompted by an Affectation of Singularity; but is, in Fact, the Result of much Reflection, and of very minute Investigation.

"To do Justice to the Subject would be to extend a *Preface* — to a Volume; but it may not be unnecessary to prove, that I have not hazarded so *bold* a Declaration on *slight* Grounds; and that, while I endeavor to convince my *Reader*, I am, at least, convinced *myself*.

"The Poetry of Dryden, though allowed to be, in *general*, Correct, Energetic, and Harmonious, is also said to be *sometimes* Careless, Languid, and Prosaic; in Fine (to use his own Words, when speaking of Milton), he is charged with having '*Flats* among his *Elevations*.[']⁶⁴ — They who *bring* the Charge usually accompany it with an Exclamation of 'how unfortunate was the *poor Man*, whose Necessities compelled him to precipitate his Works to the Press in *so unfinished* a State!'⁶⁵

"I will admit the Justice of the *Accusation*, but wave [sic], as entirely unnecesary, the *Apology*. — *Poor* he certainly was — to the never-dying Infamy of the Age which he so splendidly adorned; but his Poverty has little to do with the Question in Debate. — Many of his Lines *seem*, it is true, to have wanted his *last Touches*; but those last Touches, I am persuaded, were not *hastily* Neglected — but *deliberately* Denied. His intuitive Judgement, doubtless, suggested, that all Things figure *but* by Comparison; and that even Excellence, *undiversified*, must, at length, Fatigue. He, therefore, *subdued* his Style *occasionally* — to burst upon his Reader with *greater Splendour*, when the Subject demanded a Loftier Lay.

"But how reconcile this Supposition to his Remark respecting Milton — which seems to imply, that no Flats *should* be admitted among the Elevations?

—Very easily. — Steadiness and Consistency were, by no Means, Characteristics of the Doctrines which Dryden promulgated in his numerous
Prefaces; — Doctrines which he varied, without much Scruple as Times or
Circumstances changed: and, in the present Case, Dread of Milton's superior
Genius, and Detestation of his political Principles, might, reasonably, be
supposed somewhat to pervert his natural Candour, and somewhat to bias
his wonted Impartiality.

"The Poetry of Pope, though less enriched with [by] Classical Knowledge,
and less illumined by Vivid Imagination, appears, however, at *first* Sight, to
greater Advantage than that of Dryden; as it is, certainly, more elaborately
correct, and more mechanically *regular* — more delicately *polished*, and more
systematically *dignified*, — But are these *really* Advantages? — Let us examine.

"Does the skilful Painter bring *all* his Figures forward on the Canvas, and
bestow the last Hand upon *every* Part of the Picture?

"Does the Musician *cloy* The Ear with an eternal Succession of *harmonious*
Sounds, uncontrasted by the dire, but necessary, *Discords*?

"Does the Ornament of the Stage lavish Emphasis, Expression, Attitude,
and Action, upon *every* Line of *every* Sentence?

"Does the Beauty of a Birth-Night[66] concentrate *all* her Jewels (unrelieved
by Interstices of black Velvet) in one Intolerable Blaze?

"Would the Face of Creation appear more lovely, were it — instead of
'rising into Inequalities, diversified by the varied Exuberance of abundant
Vegetation' — to exhibit one immensurable 'Velvet Lawn, shaven by the
Scythe, and levelled by the Roller?'[67]

"Why then must Poetry adopt a preposterous Plan of *Equalisation* which
her Sister Muses reject with Scorn — and aspire to an *imaginary* perfection,
alike unknown to Nature and to Art?

"The Question seems to lie in so small a Compass, and to be so easy of
Determination, that one feels inclined to enquire how so absurd a Notion
could possibly gain a Footing, and maintain its Ground, in an Age so
polished and enlightened as to have acquired the Title of Augustan? —
Great Events, 'tis certain, arise sometimes from very trivial Causes; but
never, surely, was so important a Revolution in the *Parnassian* Realms
produced by Means so utterly contemptible!

"When Dryden's Sun was set, darting its* brightest Ray at its Departure,
Pope was beginning to dawn on the poetical Hemisphere, — A young Man of
lively Talents, with a peculiar 'Knack at Rhyming,'[68] could not fail to
attract the Notice of many would-be *Maecenases*; among others, one Walsh
undertook to usher this rising Genius into the World: he did more; he
affected to point out a Way, by which his Pupil should surpass all who had
gone before him. — 'Mr. Pope (said he), there is *one* Path as yet entirely
untrodden — the Path of *Correctness*: Dryden was a great Poet — but he had
not *Leisure* to be correct. — Seize the glorious Opportunity; supply the
Deficiency, and be immortal![']'[69]

71

"In an evil Hour did the ambitious young Bard hearken to the fatal Advice of 'knowing Walsh' (as he somewhere calls him);[70] and, hoping to supply this supposed Deficiency, he began to labour, and stiffen, and polish, and refine: till, having discarded whatever seemed loose, or languid, or harsh, or prosaic, his Verse Flowed in one equal, smooth, mellifluous Stream; marked by an almost total Want of that Variety of Pause, Accent, Cadence, and Diction, so eminently conspicuous in his incomparable Predecessor, and so absolutely essential to the Harmony of true Poetry.

"The Thought is so seldom suffered to stray beyond the Bounds of the Couplet, and so frequently wire-drawn merely to end with it — one Part of a Line so exactly reflects the other — [and] there is such a Paucity of Triplets and of Alexandrines (the Break too, in the latter, so regularly at the sixth Syllable), — that even the most ingenious Allusions, the most striking, beautiful, and graceful Imagery, the most perspicuous and pointed good Sense, and the most elegant and nervous Expression — with all their Powers united — find it difficult to render the tiresome Uniformity of his Versification supportable.

"To the officious Interposition of this same Walsh, then, we are indebted for the Contamination of the Heliconian Fountain for near a Century! Risum teneatis?[71]

"But so material a Change in the Constitution of Poetry could not be expected to take Place without some literary Convulsions. — The Disciples of Dryden were ardent in their Veneration, formidable by their Numbers, and respectable by their Rank. — Violent was the Clamour, and tedious was the Contest. — Pope, however, in the End — by Means not very honorable indeed — proved triumphant.

"In the Course of my Researches, I have found considerable Amusement (though alloyed, in no small Degree, by a Mixture of Scorn and Indignation), in tracing and developing the insidious Arts which he suffered his Friends to practise, in order to undermine the Reputation of the deceased Poet and to asperse the Characters of his living Supporters; and if a Work, which, for a longer Term of Years than that prescribed by Horace,[72] has been incarcerated in my Closet, should ever escape into Light, Pope's Goodness of Heart would be no longer problematical: — at present, I shall content myself with observing, that He, while the injured Dryden sunk in the public Estimation, was exalted to the vacant Chair, and proposed as a bright Exemplar to all succeeding Bards.

"But, as He was supposed to have improved upon his Master, Our Poets seem ambitious of improving upon theirs. — He rejected every Thing that was not rich; They reject every Thing that is not brilliant. — He is every where clear and manly; They not unfrequently torture into Obscurity, and refine into Imbecillity.

"To confirm and illustrate my Observation, by selecting Instances of harsh Construction and fantastic Inversion — Tinsel Phrases and tinkling Compound-Epithets — were a Task as easy as it were unpleasant and unwise. —

72

The *Genus irritabile Vatum*[73] is proverbial; and I shall, probably, find Inconvenience enough, from having *disturbed* the Hornet's Nest, by a General Censure, without the additional Imprudence of pulling it about my Ears by a Particular Enumeration. — Suffice it, therefore, to observe, that the *modern* System appears decisively to exclude every Mode of Expression from *Poetry* which is so unlucky as to find a Place in *Prose*.

"Let me not be misunderstood. — Poetic Diction and that Alone, is the Object of my Reprobation; nor, even in *that* Department, am I insensible of some very *splendid* Exceptions: but flatter myself, as the Influence of *their* Example gradually *expands*, that I shall still live to see the *apparent* Negligence but *real* Art — the *dignified* Simplicity — the *unaffected* Sublimity — and the *endless* Variety of the Prince of Rhyme (as Mr. Hayley justly styles him),[74] once more shine forth, in the Fullness of Beauty — the Admiration of all — but *cold, mechanical* Versifiers, and *tasteless, blind* Idolators!"[75]

I then proceed to combat Dr. Johnson's Assertion, that an Alexandrine *"invariably* requires a Break at the *sixth* Syllable;"[76] and, after endeavouring to prove that the Pause may be introduced, with considerable Effect, at the *fifth, seventh,* and *eighth* Syllables**, thus conclude the Subject:

"To multiply Instances would be superfluous; enough has been said to demonstrate what many have supposed to be incapable of Demonstration — *viz.* that Pope is not *infallible*, nor his Biographer *invulnerable*.

"If this should seem the Language of *Exultation*, let it be remembered that it is, likewise, the Language of *Conviction*; and — to repress the gathering Sneer, which an *Introduction* so disproportioned to the Size of the Poem may tempt — let ill-natured Criticism be informed, that to justify the *Style* of the following Translation is but a *subordinate* Object: my principal Design in this Prefatory Essay being to seize an apt Occasion — unexpectedly presented — of co-operating with *those* who so meritoriously endeavor to restore to Drydenical Purity that Pierian Spring which Pope *corrupted*, and which his more daring *Imitators* have Poisoned!"[77]

You will please to observe, Mr. Urban, that the Opinions which I have here expressed, when divested of their figurative Dress, are briefly these. — That Rhyme was brought by Dryden to the utmost Pitch of Perfection; that it was injured by Pope; and still *more* injured by his Successors.

The Reasons on which I ground these Opinions are stated, I am sure, with Sincerity and Candour; and, I hope, with good Manners. If they will not plead for themselves, they must stand condemned; for I have neither Health nor Spirits (as I fear I fear I have already too often hinted) to exert myself, at present, in their Support. — To Miss Seward's

Strictures, however, I have pledged myself to reply; and, in the first Place, I own that I do not readily apprehend with what Propriety Sentiments sustained by Argument *can* be styled Prejudices: but, well aware how easily a Person may be deceived, when judging of *himself*, I will not obstinately contest the Point; nay, I will freely confess that, having been, for more than twenty Years, in the *Habit* of admiring Dryden, I may, possibly, entertain a greater Predilection in his Favour than his Merit will justify. — But can my fair Opponent be *quite* certain that she is entirely free from a similar Influence with Respect to Pope?

[Weston goes on to note that "more than once," Miss Seward has misunderstood or misquoted him.]

She has produced three Lists of Authors,[78] to prove what I never denied, *viz.* that the Writers of Verses are more plentiful *now* than they were in the Days of Dryden or of Pope; and, after observing that "the last is (Milton excepted) far the brightest, as well as greatly the most numerous, of the three Lists," she demands — "have they of this third List collectively 'poisoned the Pierian Spring,' either respecting Sentiment, Imagery, or Style?"[79] — I am firmly persuaded that they *have* — with Regard to "Style;" but why must "Sentiment" and "Imagery" be introduced? — *I* had not mentioned either. — "Poetic Diction, and that alone, is the Object of my Reprobation; nor even in *that* Department am I insensible of some very *splendid* Exceptions."[80] — These were my 'Words. — Miss Seward cannot expect me to be so daringly imprudent as to specify particularly those "splendid Exceptions." — My Preface assigns a Reason for my Reluctance to select "*Instances* of harsh Construction and fantastic Inversion, Tinsel Phrases, and tinkling Compound-Epithets;" and, indeed, *were* I to be so rash, what would be the Use? — to point them out to those who *do* possess a true poetic Taste — would be unnecessary; and to those who do *not* — would be ridiculous! Who talks of Music — to the Deaf — or of Painting — to the Blind?

Miss Seward observes, that my Essay "enumerates what it calls *tinkling* Compound-Epithets amongst the fancied Improvements of the Moderns." — — "Tinkling (she adds) is a most inapplicable Adjective; since, when *ill*-chosen, Compound-Epithets may be stiff, may *grate*, but cannot *tinkle*, on the Ear. When *well*-chosen, their Merit is not to the *Ear*, but to the *Understanding* — by their condensing and energetic power."[81] — To the latter Part of this Paragraph no Objection can be made; but, with great Deference to such high Authority, I must beg Leave still to retain my Opinion, that *some* ill-chosen Compound-Epithets may Tinkle if others may Grate; and I shall, for *once*, risk a *modern* Quotation, that I may confirm my Position, and prove that I am not accustomed to deal in unfounded Assertions.

74

"Each Change of Many-colour'd Life he drew." Johnson.[82]
"Shakes o'er the darken'd Throne her Blood-distilling Plumes."
Hayley.[83]
"Glance their many-twinkling Feet." Gray.[84]

Judgement must own that the first of these Compound-Epithets is appropriative, easy, and elegant; that the second is picturesque, aweful, and sublime; and that the third is affected, *tinkling*, and nonsensical.

My candid Antagonist owns that I have convicted Prior and Montague[85] of one Mistake; but calls that Mistake *trivial.* — With Submission, it appears to *me* to be of the highest Importance. — Can she possibly suppose that the two Associates were such Blockheads, as to *believe* the Words "doomed" and "fated" were intended by Dryden to express the *same Thing?* — — If they *were* such Blockheads, they were, surely, ill qualified for Critics; and if, on the other Hand, they did *not* believe the Words to be synonymous, their Consciences must, of course, give the Lye to their Criticism. — In short (for why should I *mince* the matter?), they must be deficient in *Sense*, or in *Honesty*; and, in either Case, totally unfit for Judges! Great *indeed* must be the Abilities which can reasonably hope to extricate them from this deplorable Dilemma!

Granting the Observations, which Miss Seward has *extracted,* to be "indisputably just," it does not follow that "my Prejudice must be extreme," because I denominated their Production a "wretched Abortion of silly Malevolence." — There are but few Rules without Exceptions; and I trust that they who will take the Trouble of wading through their muddy Pamphlet will find, that the *general* Tenour of the Work will amply justify the Severity of my language.

I *did* "select the eight charming Verses, which open the Hind and Panther, as Specimens of *fine Style;*"[86] to prove that Pope did not "*heighten* the Magic of that Versification which he acknowledged to have learned from Dryden."[87] — I own that they *are* Almost "exactly in the Manner of Pope;"[88] but I think that they differ *widely* from that of his Disciples. The Lines are much too unaffected, and much too intelligible, to resemble *many* of Modern Fabrication: — I also confess that they are *not* in Dryden's *general* Manner. — Beautiful as they are, the Artfulness of their Construction is rather *too* apparent; and, had he *uniformly* written so mechanically, I should have been as much fatigued with *his* Virgil, as I have been with his *Pupil's* Homer.   Joseph Weston.

(*To be concluded in the Supplement.*)

*   Dryden's inimitable Ode is said to have been his last Production.
["Alexander's Feast; or the Power of Musique. An Ode in Honour of
St. Cecilia's Day" (1697). This is Dryden's last lyric poem. *Fables
Ancient and Modern* (1700) was his final work. See Kinsley 1: Table of
Contents.]

**   Miss Seward has inadvertently quoted me as affirming, "that the
Pause may be placed after *any* of the Syllables, without Injury to the
Harmony" [Letter 1c]. No such Affirmation appears in my Essay;
and I can only account for the Mistake, by supposing that I must
have dropped some such Remark in Conversation: for I am as
confident as I am of my Existence that Miss Seward is incapable of
intentional Misrepresentation.

8d.

Conclusion of Mr. Weston's *Reply to* Miss Seward's *Strictures on the Preface to
the* Woodmen of Arden *(from* [GM] *vol. LIX p. 1106.* [Continues Letter
8c.]

"It always appeared to me," says Miss Seward, "that Pope formed his
Style upon a few of the best passages in Dryden. Mr. W. is very angry
with him for separating the Dross from the Gold."[104] — That Pope was
indebted to Dryden for his Style, and something *more* than Style, the
astonishing number of Phrases, Half lines and Whole-lines, which he
has, most unblushingly, transferred from Dryden's Works to his own
abundantly evinces. — I am not angry with him for rejecting the
Dross — but for not admitting a Portion of Alloy, sufficient to give to his
own Coin Strength, Permanence and Currency. — That Dryden's Gold
is entirely *free* from Dross I will not be so absurd as to affirm; but,
whatever may be found reprehensible in his Sentiments or Imagery, his
Style, I will still contend, is pure. — With "incongruous Metaphor" and
"inconsistent Fable"[105] I meddle not; my business is merely with his
Diction.

Miss Seward allows that Pope too generally confines the Sense within
the Boundary of the Couplet; but thinks that Dryden permits it to
overflow too often, and that he is too fond of Iambics. — Though *I* think
otherwise, I know of no argument which can establish as a *Fact* what, I
fear, must remain Matter of *Opinion*; and I have Humility enough to
recollect Whose Opinion it is, from which I am so unfortunate as to
dissent.

She further observes that Pope "uses the spirited Accent upon the first syllable in a Verse twenty Times for once that it occurs in Dryden;" and that the Verses of the "former describe in the lively dramatic *present* Tense much oftener than the latter."[106] — These assertions I feel no inclination to controvert; perfectly satisfied that my cautious Opponent *examined* before she *affirmed*. — I allow that Alexandrines are not *often* graceful in the *Middle* of Sentences; but I shall presently have occasion to produce an Exception to this Rule. — Why She, who reasons so ably on the *condensing* Power of Compound-Epithets, should conceive such a dislike to Dryden's Triplets, I do not readily comprehend; since the Latter assuredly possess *that* Power, in an eminent Degree: compressing into *three* Lines the Sense which, though refusing to be confined within *two*, would become too much enfeebled were it wire-drawn into *four*; not to mention the additional Dignity which the majestic Alexandrine Derives, from being preceded by *two* Relatives, instead of *one*.

The Quotation from the Iliad, in Point of picturesque Harmony, may have been rivalled, but will never be excelled. — But why contrast this utmost effort of Pope's long-practised Wing with the first weak attempt of Dryden's unfledged Pinion? — That the Genius of Pope was at its Zenith, at an Age when that of Dryden was yet below the Horizon, is granted. — And what then? — The Former (in the Opinion of Dr. Johnson,[107] at least,) never exceeded his *Essay on Criticism*, written at Seventeen; and the Latter (in the Opinion of all the World) never equalled his incomparable *Music Ode* — produced at Seventy! — A Reflection not very much to the Advantage of the *Premature* Poet!

If Dryden, in his eighteenth Year, afforded such faint Glimmerings of that Poetic Flame which afterward blazed so bright, what Hope would Miss Seward have entertained of the celebrated Jonathan Swift, had she seen his first Performance in *Verse*, (if it deserves the Name,) when he was twenty-four years old — from which the following extracts are taken?

> "The first of Plants after the Thunder, Storm, and Rain,
> And thence with joyful, nimble Wing,
> Flew dutifully back again.
> Who by that, vainly talks of baffling Death,
> And hopes to lessen Life, by a Transfusion of Breath.
> And seen (almost) transform'd to Water, Flame, and Air,
> So well you answer all Phaenomenas there."
>
> *Anecdotes ancient and modern,*
> *By James Petit Andrews, F. A. S.* page 295.[108]

77

Miss Seward proceeds to select six or seven Lines from Juno's Soliloquy, in the first Book of the Aeneid; to prove "that Dryden, in his *riper* Years, was prone to let his Style fall below the poetic Level, where the Subject called *aloud* for Elevation."[109] — To prove that he does not, however, fall below his *Original* will, I apprehend, be deemed ample justification — Permit me, therefore, Mr. Urban, to copy the *whole* Speech from Virgil, to subjoin a *literal* Version (for the Information of such of your Readers as may have neglected their Latin) and then to add the Translation in Question.

> — — Me-ne incepto desistere victam?
> Nec posse Italia Teucrorum avertere regem?
> Quippe vetor fatis. Pallas-ne exurere classem,
> Argivum, atque ipsos potuit submergere ponto,
> Unius ob noxam & furias Ajacis Oilei?
> Ipsa Jovis rapidum jaculata e nubibus ignem,
> Disjecitque rates, evertitque aequora ventis:
> Illum exspirantem transfixo pectore flammas
> Turbine corripuit, scopuloque infixit acuto.
> Ast ego, quae Divum incedo regina, Jovisque
> Et soror, & conjux, una cum gente tot annos
> Bella gero; & quisquam numen Junonis adoret
> Praeterea, aut supplex aris imponat honorem?
>
> [*Aeneid* 1:36-48.]

Must I, overpowered, desist from my enterprise? And cannot I drive the Trojan King from Italy? I am forbidden by the Fates, forsooth! Could Pallas burn the *Fleet* of the Greeks, and drown *them* in the Sea, for the Crime of one *alone* — for the mad Passion of Ajax Oileus? She hurled the rapid Fire of Jupiter from the Clouds, and shattered the Ships, and* turned the Sea up from the Bottom with the Winds, and seized him with a Whirlwind, *expiring* Flames from his transfixed Breast, and fastened him to a pointed Rock — But I, who walk the Queen of the Gods, both the sister and the Wife of Jove, wage War so many years with *one* Nation; and who will, hereafter, adore the power of Juno, or, suppliant, place Honours on her Altar?

> Then am I *vanquish'd*, must I yield, said she,
> And *must* the Trojans reign in Italy?
> So Fate *will* have it, and Jove adds his Force;
> Nor can my Power *divert* their happy Course.
> Cou'd angry *Pallas*, with revengeful Spleen,
> The Grecian Navy *burn*, and *drown* the Men?
> She, for the Fault of *one* offending Foe,

The Bolts of Jove Himself *presum'd* to throw:
With Whirlwinds from beneath she toss'd the Ship,
And bare expos'd the Bosom of the Deep:
Then, *as an eagle gripes the trembling Game,*
The Wretch *yet hissing with her Father's Flame.*
She strongly seiz'd, and, with a burning wound
Transfix'd, *and naked,* on a Rock she bound.
But I, who walk in *awful State* above,
†*The Majesty of Heav'n,* the Sister-Wife of Jove,
For Length of Years my *fruitless* Force employ
Against *the thin Remains of ruin'd Troy.*
What Nations now to Juno's Pow'r will pray,
Or Off'rings on my *slighted* Altars lay? [*Ae* 3:1.56-75.]

If Miss Seward's Observation, in your Magazine for September, (page 820)[110] be just — viz. that "the only Plan which can make Translations worth any thing is — to abandon every idea of closeness, and to *interweave any new Sentiment or Imagery* that occurs, if it can add Grace or Spirit to the Theme" — then will this masterly Translation procure for its Author "the Honours of *original Composition;*" the English will be found, on Comparison, *nowhere* Inferior, and in *many* Places greatly Superior to the Latin.

My facetious Antagonist laughs at the *Hissing* which the poor Devil made, whom the Heavenly Virago sous'd *redhot* into the Sea; and adverts to Shakespear's Jolly Knight and his Buckbasket: but I must beg leave to decline being a partaker of the Merriment — it shall be proved that the expression is *inapplicable,* and until I shall be convinced that Wit and Humour have lost their acknowledged prerogative, of making *any* Phrase, however just, however pertinent, appear ridiculous, for a Time — by exhibiting it in a ludicrous Point of View, or by contriving for it an unlucky association.

But Sense *survives,* when merry Jests are *past,*[111]

Apropos. — What a glorious Use has the ingenious Critic made of the Coalition of Dryden with Lord Mulgrave,[112] in a translation from Ovid![113] — Nor can I blame her. — The Cause which she had undertaken to support required *every* Exertion of her multifarious Pen; and *no* Expedient that was not absolutely disingenuous was to be *rejected:* (for of Disingenuousness I know her to be incapable). — Stratagems are lawful in a poetical as well as in a political Warfare; and though it was impossible that Sagacity like *hers* could, for one Moment, be imposed upon by the Lustre of a *Name* — though She could not *but* be sensible that

79

the Translator of the Epistle from Canace to Macareus, and of that from Dido to Aeneas, *could not possibly* scribble one Line of that paltry Stuff which she has extracted from Helen's Epistle to Paris — she certainly was not obliged to render that Justice to Dryden which he did not think proper to claim — nay, which he actually renounced. — As he suffered his Credit to be so shamefully prostituted, for the mean Purpose of tickling the Vanity of a rhyming Peer, he well deserved the disgrace of having that meagre and ricketty Brat, to which he acted the Part of *Midwife* as well as of *Father*, brought forward, as a Foil to the beautiful and elegant offspring of his more prudent Competitor.

By the Way, how are we to prove, unless by *internal* Evidence, whether Dryden *did* — or did *not* — write the Lines in Dispute? — The right Honourable the Earl of Mulgrave's Name appears to the *Firm* of the *House.* — How are we to ascertain, with Precision, *what* Share each contributed to the joint-stock, unless by comparing, Article by Article, the various Kinds of Goods thus strangely jumbled together, with the *very* different Qualities of *those* fabricated in the respective Manufactories which *each* of the quondam Associates established, after the preposterous Partnership was dissolved?

Upon the Ground of *this* Species of Examination, I may venture to affirm (without the slightest Hazard of Contradiction from any one possessed of discriminating Taste) that Mulgrave was the Author of every Syllable of the Translations from Ovid, which Miss Seward has ascribed to Dryden.

This *Mezentian* Combination,[114] this unnatural junction of the *living* with the *dead*, provoked the Waggery of contemporary Wits. — One Couplet I recollect.

> "How [But how] did [could] this *learned Brace* employ their Time?
> "One *construed* sure — while t'other *pump'd for Rhyme!*"[115]

The pecuniary Advantages which the *Poet* might reap from his Connexion with the *Lord* (and they surely must have been *great*, to atone for *such* a Sacrifice!) were not without their Alloy. — The abandon'd and cowardly Rochester hired Ruffians to cudgel Dryden, in Revenge for an admirable Portrait of him, in the Essay on Satire; a Work in which Mulgrave was *again* permitted to claim a Share.[116] — If the peer may be believed, (but no Judge of Poetry *can* believe him) the Laureat was "prais'd and beaten for another's Rhymes."[117] — No, no, Lord Mulgrave *We* know better; and *Rochester* knew better. — Aut Erasmus aut Diabolus.[118] — The Cudgel was certainly applied to the *Author* of the Rhymes. If Dryden's Poverty and Pope's Avarice induced them to lavish upon you unmerited Honours, for which Posterity will pity one and despise the other, as much as *I* do — your Lordship's critical and poetical abilities, rest assured, (in spite of their lying Praises,) are beneath all Contempt!

I cannot, Mr. Urban, forbear smiling at the Slyness with which Pope, while affecting to commend this same Earl of Mulgrave for that Miserable Farrago of common-place Cant, called the *Art of Poetry*,[119] carefully points out the vilest Line *among* the vile — as an Example of its Excellence.

"Nature's *chief* Master-piece — is Writing well." [*EOC* 1:724][120]

[Weston elaborates on the badness of Mulgrave's "water-gruel" poetry.]

In short — the right Honourable the Earl of Mulgrave was, meo periculo,[121] the Doer of the *second* Version of Dido's Epistle to Aeneas![122] —Let the *Doubtful* compare the uniform Style of *that* with "Helen to Paris ††."

As a striking Proof of the Superiority of Dryden, not only to his contemptible Coadjutor, but also to his elegant Original, give me Leave, Mr. Urban, to present your Readers with the *Conclusion* of the Epistle, as it appears in Ovid — in Mulgrave — and in Dryden! accompanied by a close Translation, for the Reason before assigned.

> Pro meritis, & siqua tibi debebimus ultro,
>   Pro spe conjugii tempora parva peto,
> Dum freta mitescunt & amor: dum tempore & usu
>   Fortiter edisco tristia posse pati.
> Sin minus; est animus nobis effundere vitam.
>   In me crudelis non potes esse diu.
> Adspicias utinam, quae sit scribentis imago!
>   Scribimus; & gremio Troicus ensis adest:
> Perque genas lacrymae strictum labuntur in ensem;
>   Qui jam pro lacrymis sanguine tinctus erit.
> Quam bene conveniunt fato tua munera nostro!
>   Instruis impensa nostra sepulcra brevi.
> Nec mea nunc primo feriuntur pectora telo:
>   Ille locus saevi vulnus Amoris habet.
> Anna soror, soror Anna, meae male conscia culpae,
>   Jam dabis in cineres ultima dona meos.
> Nec, consumta rogis, inscribar Elissa Sichaei;
>   Hoc tamen in tumuli marmore carmen erit:
> Praebuit Aeneas & causam mortis & ensem
>   Ipsa sua Dido concidit usa manu.[123]

81

On account of what I have merited, and if *I* am to be indebted to thee for any voluntary Kindness, on Account of my Hope of Marriage, I implore a little Time; until the Seas and my affections grow calm: until by Time and Habit I learn to bear my Sorrows with Fortitude. But if *not* — I am resolved to shed my Blood. Thou canst not be cruel to me long. I wish thou could'st witness my Appearance while writing! I write; and in my Lap lies the Trojan Sword: and Tears glide down my Cheeks upon the drawn Blade; which will instantly be stained with Blood instead of Tears. How well thy Gifts agree with my Fate! Thou preparest my Sepulchre at a small Expence. Nor is my Breast now pierced with the *first* Weapon: that place already bears the Wound of cruel Love! ** Oh Anna! O my sister! Unhappily conscious of my Crime! Thou wilt soon pay the last Tribute to my Ashes. Nor, when consumed on the Funeral pile, will I be styled Sichaeus's Elissa; but this Verse shall be on the Marble of my Tomb: "Aeneas supplied both the *Motive* of Death, and the Sword. Dido fell by her own Hand."

Mulgrave's Translation.

By all I suffer, all I've done for you,
Some little Respite to my Love allow.
Time and Calm Thoughts may teach me how to bear
That Loss, which now alas 'tis Death to hear,
But you resolve to force me to my Grave,
And are not far from all that you would have.
Your Sword before me, whilst I write, does lye,
And by it, if I write in vain, I die.
Already stain'd with many a falling Tear,
It shortly shall another Colour wear.
You never could an apter Present make,
'Twill soon the Life you made uneasy take.
But this poor Breast has felt your Wounds before,
Slain by your Love, your Steel has now no Pow'r.
Dear guilty sister, do not you deny
The last kind office to my Memory;
But do not on my Fun'ral Marble join
Much wrong'd Sichaeus' sacred Name with mine.
"Of false Aeneas let the Stone complain;
"That Dido could not bear his fierce Disdain,
"But by his Sword, and her own Hand was slain.["]

Dryden's Translation.

If by no *Merit* I thy mind can move,
What thou deny'st my merit give my *Love*.
Stay 'till I *learn* my Loss to undergo;
And give me Time to *struggle* with my Woe.
If *not*: know This, I will not suffer *long*,
My Life's too *loathsome*, and my Love too *strong*.
Death Holds My Pen, and *dictates what I say*,
While cross my Lap the [thy] Trojan Sword I lay.
My Tears flow down; the *sharp* Edge cuts their Flood,
And drinks my *Sorrows*, that must drink my *Blood*
How well thy Gift does with my Fate agree!
My Fun'ral pomp is cheaply made by thee.
To no *new* Wounds my Bosom I display:
The *Sword* But enters where *Love* Made the Way.
But thou, dear Sister, *and yet dearer Friend,*
Shalt my *cold* Ashes to their Urn attend.
Sichaeus' Wife let not the Marble boast,
I lost that Title when my Fame I lost.
This short Inscription only let it bear,
"Unhappy Dido lyes in *Quiet* Here.
"The *Cause* of Death, and *Sword* by which she dy'd
"Aeneas gave: The *rest* her arm supply'd." [DA 1:191-212.]

I am, at length, arrived at Miss Seward's third and last Letter....

* * * *

I only rejected the Apology commonly made for Dryden (viz. Poverty) because I thought and continue to think it unnecessary. — I am still firmly of Opinion that — whatever Alterations a deliberate Revisal of his hasty Publications might have produced, in his Images and Sentiments, his Style would have remained untouched; its striking Inequality being, I sincerely believe, the Result of Choice rather than of Necessity. — Having sufficiently discussed this Point, in my Preface, I shall content myself with producing an Authority in my Favour, which Miss Seward, I am sure, will acknowledge to be highly worthy of Attention.

In Warton's celebrated Essay on the Genius and Writings of Pope, (Vol. ii. p. 175.) after some Remarks on the well-known Lines on the Man Of Ross,[124] the learned and ingenious Writer thus proceeds.

"The particular Reason for which I quoted them, was to observe the pleasing Effect that the Use of common and familiar Words and Objects, judiciously managed, produce in Poetry. Such as are here the Words,

Causeway, Seats, Spire, Market-place, Alms-house, apprentic'd. A fastidious Delicacy, and a false Refinement, in order to avoid Meanness, have deterred our Writers from the Introduction of such Words; but Dryden often hazarded it, and gave by it a secret Charm, and a natural Air to his Verses, well knowing of what Consequence it was sometimes to soften and subdue his Tints, and not to paint and adorn every Object he touched, with perpetual Pomp and unremitted Splendor."[125]

Your polite Correspondent M — — s (to whom I am indebted for a very handsome Compliment) either had not read, or had forgotten this remarkable paragraph, when he expressed an Apprehension that I should not, perhaps, find a single Advocate for what he, inattentively, styles my "Assertion" — though I had, in Fact, only given it as my *Opinion.*

I certainly *have* attacked Pope's moral Character, and shall as certainly make good my Charge; but I cannot recollect that I have *praised* that of Dryden, and, therefore, am not compelled to defend it from Miss Seward's weighty Accusations. — Strongly tempted, however, to extenuate, in some Degree, such Parts of his erroneous Conduct as will *admit* of Extenuation, Fear of lenghtening that which is already too long *alone* restrains my Pen.

Had I not been convinced by a very serious Investigation, that the Disposition of Pope was *base and rancorous* in the Highest Degree, and that his*** Example has been attended with pernicious effects, his Memory would have remain undisturbed by Me. — I never heard that he "relieved the necessities of his abusive Foe"[126] otherwise than by† writing a delightful Prologue to a Play[127] acted for the Benefit of the poor old Man, after he had lost his sight; unless a couple of Guineas which he paid, as a Subscription, for two Volumes of Epistolary Correspondence, which Dennis published,[128] may be placed to the Account of Charity.

They who shall peruse the following Letter, written by Pope, though (for very *wise* Reasons) not inserted in his *own* artful and mutilated Edition of his Works,[129] may possibly attribute his seeming Liberality to a Motive less exalted than that suggested by his generous Apogolist.

To Mr. Dennis.

Sir,   May 3, 1721.

I called to receive the two Books of your Letters from Mr. Congreve, and have left with him the *little Money* I am in your Debt. I look upon myself to be Much More So, *for the Omissions you have been pleased to make* [*in those Letters*] *in my Favour,* and sincerely join with you in the Desire that *not the* Least *Traces may remain of that Difference between us, which indeed* I Am Sorry For. You may therefore believe me, without either *Ceremony* or *Falseness*, Sir, Your most obedient humble Servant,

A. Pope.[130]

* * * *

In treating of the Alexandrine, Miss Seward has been witty, if not argumentative;[131] but, indeed, Argument has but little to do in the business. The proper Places for the *Break* must, after all, be settled by the Ear; and, having appropriated so many Pages of my Essay to the Elucidation of this subject, I think any addition to my former Remarks superfluous.

When I mentioned "Wou'd be Maecenases"[132] I alluded to Hallifax, Buckingham, Walsh, and the rest of the "Mob of Gentlemen, who wrote with Ease,"[133] and prated about Poetry and Criticism; undignified by Genius, and unadorned by Taste: — of Walsh I have spoken, in my Preface; Buckingham's Pretensions may be nearly ascertained, from the Specimens which I have adduced; and they, who (unsatisfied by my Quotation from the City Mouse and the Country Mouse) are curious to learn yet more of the *critical* Talents which Hallifax possessed, may obtain *entire* Satisfaction, by referring to an Anecdote, of unquestionable Authenticity, related in Dr. Johnson's Life of Pope.[134] — Surely I could not intend to discourage Poetic Patronage, in an age like *this* that seems to plume itself on patronizing *every* Art liberal and illiberal *except* Poetry.

Have I *really* written "as if the Excellence or Worthlessness of a Poem depended wholly upon the Construction of its Measure; and as if the Couplet was the only order of Rhyme?"[135] I must then have written in my Sleep — and am not yet awake; for I have searched, with the most rigid Scrutiny, for a single Passage that could, by any mode of Construction, be supposed to convey such a Meaning — but searched in vain. — I have said *much* about Diction, 'tis true, and *little* about any thing else; because Diction, and that alone, was my Object. But, so far from thinking Measure the *only* Essential, I cordially agree with Miss Seward, that "a Poem has little Merit if it does not remain fine Poetry after having been taken out of *all* Measure;"[136] and Horace must have been of the same Opinion: or he would scarcely have recommended the Transposition and Inversion of the Order of the Words, as a Criterion, by which to distinguish whether the Compositions (thus deprived of Measures and Numbers) contained the vital essence of Poetry![137]

* * * *

Joseph Weston.

---

* ———Up from the Bottom turn'd
By furious Winds. Milton. [*Paradise Lost* 7.213.]

† Does not the unexpected Length of this Line convey to the *Ear* a very lively Idea of the Empress of Heaven, swelling with self-importance?

And does not this Example prove that an Alexandrine *may* sometimes be introduced with Propriety in the *Middle* of a Sentence?

†† That the Author of *one* Version was perfectly conversant with the *other* the Number of Lines which bear strong Marks of Imitation incontestably prove. — To select only two Instances —

> "So, on Maeander's Banks, when Death is nigh,
> *"The mournful Swan sings her own Elegy."* Dryden.   [*DA* 1:1-2]

> "So in unwonted Notes, when sure to die
> *"The mournful Swan sings her own Elegy."* Mulgrave.

Perfect Resemblance, Mr. Urban!

> "But now with Northern Blasts the Billows roar,
> "And drive the Floating Sea-Weed to the shore." Dryden.
>   [*DA* 1:186-7]

> "These Winds have driv'n the Floating Sea-Weed so,
> "That your intangled Vessel cannot go." Mulgrave.

"Levis" — which *Both* have agreed to render "floating" — signifies *light*. — The Lightness of the Sea-Weed is, undoubtedly, the *Cause* of its floating; but — that two Persons, translating the some Word, and ignorant of each other's Intention, should *hit* upon the same elegant Mode of substituting the Effect *for* the Cause, exceeds *my* Portion of Credulity! — 'Twas no *casual* Coincidence. — The Translators were well acquainted, and had compared Notes, 'tis plain.

** "O Anna my Sister! O my sister Anna! would have been rather a ludicrous — though certainly a literal — Translation of "Anna soror, soror Anna." — Thompson [James Thomson] must surely have had this passage in his Eye, when he ventured upon that tragic Line which made his audience so merry! "Oh Sophonisba! Sophonisba Oh!" [*The Tragedy of Sophonisba* (Dublin, 1730) III. ii. 19.]

*** A more *ample* Explanation of my meaning would *here* occupy too much Room; and may not improperly be reserved till the "Ides of March:" [Shakespeare, *Julius Caesar* 1.2.18] at which Time I intend to answer the Challege of M.F. respecting the uncourtly Epithet which I applied to Pope.

††† Though it may appear somewhat invidious to assign to a good Action an unamiable Motive, I cannot help suspecting that there might be more of Parade than of Humanity in the Case. — Vanity *less* enormous than that which fell to *his* Share might have grasp'd

with Greediness at so lucky an opportunity of purchasing a very valuable Species of Fame at a very trifling Expence.

9.

Mr. Urban,   *Birmingham. Jan.* 20. [1790]

My interference in the literary engagement between Miss Seward and Mr. Weston will not, I hope, be imputed to improper views. In my prefatory advertisement to the Woodmen of Arden, I alledged that "the judicious sentiments contained in Mr. Weston's manly essay, which accompanied it, chiefly prompted me to submit to the public eye, what was originally intended for a private circle." The approbation which I then gave, justice stimulates me now to support. Mr. W. I am certain, neither wishes, nor wants, my assistance: I am well acquainted with the extent of his reading, the vigour of his intellect, the correctness of his taste, and his persevering, though candid, firmness. Animated by the cause of justice and truth, though he may be *dazzled*, he will not be *dismayed*, by the "celestial Panoply"[89] of his fair antagonist. As for myself, I feel no terrors in encountering the formidable Miss Seward: her very censure will give celebrity. But I will not praise her. Panegyric is exhausted upon the varied excellence of her character; and I have no leisure to collect the scattered sweets. It is useless to "gild refined gold, or cast a perfume on the violet." — [90]

Your correspondents M——s and M.F. are well entitled to the attention of the public; but I beg leave to confine myself to your two leaders in this interesting dispute.

With respect to Dryden and Pope, I feel no inclination to join the*
AEgyptian Inquest that has for some time been sitting on their moral characters. Dryden might be lax in his *religious*, and flexible in his *political* principles: Pope might be querulous, petulent, envious, malignant. The former might be meanly lavish of his praise, and the latter shamefully prodigal of his abuse, crying, like his parrot, "*Cuckold*" to every man in the street.[91] But the one might plead in his excuse the *malesuada fames*,[92] the almost irresistable persuasions of penury; and the latter, his natural, and perhaps incurable, irritability of disposition, inflamed by perpetual disease. It may not be improper on this occasion to quote the reply of Lord Bolingbroke, when appealed-to [sic] respecting the avarice of the celebrated Duke of Marlborough: "He was so great a man, I have forgot his faults."[93] "C'est une consolation," says Voltaire, "pour un esprit aussi borné que le mien, d'etre bien persuadé, que grands hommes se trompent comme le vulgaire."[94] —

As to the political [poetical][95] merits of the rival bards, I am compelled to give the palm to Dryden. I admit the general inequality of his poems, the occasional coldness of his conceptions, and the not unfrequent depressions of his style. I allow that he sometimes sinks lower than Pope; but he sinks to rise proportionably higher, and, like *Antaeus*, gathers strength from touching the ground.

I am abundantly convinced from the philosophy of the human mind, that without contrast and variety, the greatest intellectual efforts fail of their effect. This principle, Mr. Weston justly observes, pervades the whole circle of the fine arts: it also governs our corporeal sensations. We must fall below safe to rise above it: "The Indian Sickens amidst his grove of fragrance;"[96] and a perpetual spring, however it may charm in the page of poetry, would be intolerable. The ever-darting polish of Pope hurts my eye; his *cuckoo* notes disgust my ear; the interminable level tires; and I pant for hill and dale.

I know not whether the *sinkings* in Dryden proceeded from *neglect, accident,* or *design*; I speak merely of the *effect*, without being capable of assigning the *cause*. Some of them undoubtedly took their rise from the infirmity of the human mind. The highest flights of genius necessarily produce a temporary languor: the lark, after soaring in the clouds, reposes in the furrow.

Miss Seward seems to reason from *parts*, and Mr. W. from the *whole*; and I am convinced, from my personal knowledge of the former, that she does great violence to her feelings in the mode of conducting this dispute. It is certainly repugnant to her usual candour, to expose the dirty alleys, and neglected passages, in a magnificent city, and industriously hide from view its spacious streets, splendid squares, and "gorgeous palaces."[97] —

Longinus, in enumerating the sources of the sublime, mentions in the first place, an elevation of mind which makes us think nobly and happily; and in the second, the natural vehemence or enthusiasm which strikes and moves us. These, says he, are the gifts of nature;[98] and in these Dryden seems to me to have the advantage over Pope. Figurative language and the arrangement of words are the province of *art*. Miss S. with ingenious anxiety, endeavours to *confound* what Mr. W. wishes to separate. The question which he agitates, is not whether Dryden is more chaste and congruous in his figures than Pope, but whether he is not on the whole superior in the effect produced by the structure of his verse. And, upon the whole I agree with Mr. Weston, though I think Dryden too licentious in the use of his *Alexandrines*, particularly in the middle of sentences. When properly managed, they add much to the sonorous swell of English rhyme, and bring it nearer to the majesty of the Greek and Latin *Hexameter*, which contains no less than seventeen syllables. *Triplets* certainly do not deserve the opprobrious epithet "botching:"[99] they tend to relieve a painful uniformity, and are of singular use in translations. To make the sense invariably terminate with the couplet, which is Pope's constant manner, not only imposes unnecessary fetters on rhyme, but loses that bewitching undulation of sound, which winds through the pages of Milton, and is the same to the ear as the "magic curve of beauty to the eye."[100] I allow blank verse admits of it with greater facility, and to a greater extent than rhyme; but I would not have the latter entirely discard a grace, for the absence of which no regularity can atone. With some of the points discussed by the two contending critics, the understandng has nothing to do; but an appeal lies to the ear only. [For] my own part, I cannot read 200 pages of Pope together, without satiety: the *De gustibus non est disputandum*. The *formal cut* of the verse disgusts one like the Dutch taste in gardening, [*sic*] Nothing can be more irksome to my ear, than the lullaby occasioned by the *caesura* falling so frequently on the 4th and 5th syllable. The mellifluous melodies put me in the situation of a man half smothered with roses. No one, says Lord Kames, contracts a constant habit of taking honey.[101]

But I have lain "on these primrose beds too long:"[102] the fascinating smiles of poetry cannot long detain me from severer studies.

> "Discedam, explebo numerum, reddarque tenebris."[103]

J. Morfitt.

---

* Diodorus Siculus tells us, that it was a custom in AEgypt, for judges to sit on every man's life at his interment. [*Diodorus of Sicily*, trans. C. H. Oldfather (NY: Putnam, 1933) 1:313-15.]

10.

Mr. Urban,   *Lichfield, Feb.* 13. [1790]

Polite as are my ingenious Drydenic antagonists, I must, in justice to myself, disavow a sensibility which Mr. Morfitt affects to take for granted, and a stratagem for which Mr. Weston affects to forgive me. I have suppressed *no* sensibilities during my investigation of this subject. I scorn to suppress involuntary consciousness because it may militate against my argument. For the imputed stratagem, my combat with prejudices of such *demonstrable* futility, could not *need* the aid of auxiliary stratagem; and were it possible to have *wanted*, I would have disdained to *use* it. Solemnly do I disavow the least suspicion that the Epistle from Helen to Paris was not *his* whose name is prefixed to it. No one, impartial enough to be disgusted with bold and vulgar style in a favourite author, and who has read all Dryden's works, *can* feel *internal evidence* that a work is not *his*, which bears his name, because it is written *ill*.

I did no violence to my feelings in producing instances of wretched style in the great, the illustrious Dryden, because the nature of my dispute with Mr. W. *obliged* me to produce them, and because I thought it incumbent upon me, though he acts otherwise by Pope, to bring my *proofs with my accusations*. As *great*, as *illustrious*, with all his sins against sincerity and poetic elegance, I have ever considered Dryden; as such I have *mentioned* him through the whole course of those strictures, which defend the pointed, polished, and harmonious style of Pope, and the judgment with which he shunned whatever was turgid or vulgar in its conception, false or absurd in its metaphoric sense, awkward or slovenly in its expression.

Mr. Morfitt confesses that Dryden's imagination, which, by allusion, he justly terms a "magnificent city,"[138] has its *dirty alleys* and *neglected passages*, but thinks it uncandid to search them out. Never had they been searched out by *me*, if his friend had not publickly denied their existence in any such squalid form, and falsely termed them well-disposed shades amidst lights, and judicious flats amidst elevations; if he had not *renounced* all pardon extended to Dryden for the frequent defects of his style, on the score of pecuniary necessity; and if I had not apprehended a possibility of mischief to our young writers from Mr. Weston's erroneous assertions — mischief, that Mr. Morfitt will find stated in a letter of mine to M — — s, in the Gentleman's Magazine for September last, p. 818.[139]

To *prevent* such mischief, and without a wish to rob Dryden of those luxuriant laurels, won by the rich fertility of his ideas, by the frequent grandeur of his conceptions, and by the frequent mellifluence of his numbers, did I *prove* that they *were* blind alleys, and lamentably neglected passages in the magnificent city. I sought *not* to hide, as Mr. Morfitt more than insinuates I did, its spacious streets, splendid squares, and gorgeous palaces. Have I not said that Dryden trusted to the majestic trees of his wilderness, "laden with blooming gold,"[140] for the preservation of his fame? Was *that* the language of one who sought to *suppress* the recollection of his excellences? But I here repeat a conviction, which I sincerely feel, namely that he never dreamed that their fruits should so far intoxicate the brain of a Brother Poet, as to make him assert the superior beauty of the wilderness on *account* of its weeds, and abuse the majestic parks and lawns of succeeding Bards, from which the nettles and switch-grass have been rooted up. Flats amidst elevations do certainly promote the general beauty of the scene; but it is very undesirable that they should be overgrown with weeds, "unsightly, and unsmooth."[141] I have asserted that Pope's poetry is not destitute of this contrasting plainness and simplicity of style. It may be found in sufficient plenty in his Epistles, in his Essay on Man, on Criticism, on Fame; in his Iliad; still more in his Odyssey; and even in the glowing, impassioned, and highly-coloured poem, the Eloisa to Abelard.

If in this disquisition I have produced parts, (and what *but* parts *could* I produce?) I have judged from the *whole* — thus — that Dryden was in the *lyric* style greater than Pope, but inferior to him in that of the ten feet couplet. I acknowledged that it was a fault in the latter so *seldom* to float his pause into the middle of the next line; but that Dryden's floating it *too often*, his Alexandrines in the middle of sentences, his perpetual triplets, which hurt the ear by prolonging the jingle of the rhyme, his everlasting expletives, with which, in particular, his elegy on Cromwell is so much deformed, his "*says hes*, and *says shes* [sic]," instance:

> The Panther smil'd at this, and when *said she*
> Were these first councils disallow'd by me?

and again:

> Why all this war [these wars] to win the book, if we
> Must not interpret for ourselves *but she?*
> *Hind and Panther.*   [2:2.168-69, 283-84]

That these, I mean the habitual use of these, formed in the opposite scale of defect so much an heavier preponderance, as to give the superiority, in point of diction, clearly to Pope. I produced my *proofs* that Dryden often wrote *too* ill to write *so* ill from any other motive than necessitous haste.

Mr. Morfitt observes that "figurative language, and the arrangement of numbers, are the province of *art.*" The *latter* certainly; but the *former*, if *justly* figurative, is the constituent, the vital principle of *Genius*, that combination of remote resemblances, whose *happy* union mere art will strive to effect in *vain*. When Shakespear, describing a summer night, exclaims:

> How sweet the moonlight *sleeps* upon the bank![142]

and says that it tips with *silver* the tops of the fruit-trees;[143] and, in painting wintry darkness, tells us,

> Now the loud howling wolves arouse the hours [jades],
> That drag the tragic, melancholy night,
> And, with their drowsy, slow, and flagging wings,
> Clip dead men's graves;[144]

he speaks *figuratively*, but with *such* figures as art alone had *never* brought him.

That Dryden perpetually sinks below, O how *much* below Pope! I willingly agree with Mr. Morfitt; but that he ever rises *proportionably* higher I utterly deny, and would undertake to equal the noblest and most beautiful passages from Dryden's poems, in the couplet measure, with selections from those of his rival. Their genius was equal; but Pope would not abuse his talents, and Dryden lived in the perpetual prostitution of *his*.

That ear must be oddly modeled, to which Pope's harmonious and flowing verses appear formal. It is not allowed to the couplet rhyme to wind the pause through whole passages, as Mr. Morfitt beautifully expresses it. *Dryden* did not attempt it. *That* grace belongs to blank verse, as he allows. Hence the superiority of *exquisite* blank verse to the *most* exquisite rhyme.

Mr. Morfitt calls Pope's numbers *"Cuckoo-notes;"* if he had termed them *Blackbird* notes, he had spoke more justly; since the blackbird's, sweet beyond a name, and beyond all power of satiety to a musical ear, have *not* the varieties of the nightingale's melodies. Neither does the couplet measure admit great *variety* in the flow of the numbers; *that* grace belongs to Ode-writing, and to blank verse.

With *such* "Cuckoo-notes" as the following, I confess myself incapable of being cloyed, or of perceiving in them any resemblance to folding doors, or to Dutch gardening:

> So Zembla's rocks, the beauteous work of frost,
> Rise high [white] in air, and glitter on the coast;
> Pale suns [unfelt] at distance roll unfelt away,
> And on th' impassive ice the lightnings play.
> Eternal snows the growing mass supply,
> Till the bright mountains prop th' incumbent sky:
> Like [As] Atlas fix'd each hoary pile appears
> The gather'd winter of a thousand years. [*TF* 2:53-60.]

Pope's severity to the Dunces, who had maligned him, was *just* chastisement. They *gave* the provocation; they distilled their venom upon his immortal laurels, though it had no power to canker them. He formed a mock-heroic poem in consequence of thei[r] malice, and made his enemies ridiculous to all ages. Such ever be the doom of Envy aspersing Virtue, and endeavouring to shroud the light of Genius!

Mr. Weston still procrastinates his *proofs*, that Pope was an execrable villain, the insidious underminer of *his* fame, whom he professed to honour. My antagonist has closed the correspondence with me, without producing them. He owed it to his own character, and to the demand I made upon him for those proofs, to have produced them in the *first* page of his reply. To assert Dryden's style *advantaged* by its frequent vapidness and vulgarity, is *but* want of taste for pure and elegant composition. From *unsupported* accusation, brought against the *moral character* of a fine writer, every one will turn indignant, who can feel his beauties, and be grateful for the delights they have afforded.

Ere I make any comments upon Mr. Weston's letter in the last Magazine,[145] where every position he advances is open to confutation, I shall wait the promissory Ides of March for those proofs which my friendship for Mr. Weston almost induces me to wish he may be *able* to produce. It behooves him to take especial care that they be *unquestionable*.

Yours, &c. Anna Seward.

11.

Mr. Urban, *Oct.* 11. [1789]

I am much flattered by the notice which your fair correspondent ([*GM*] vol. LIX. p. 820)[146] has paid to my remarks on her poetical strictures*: but, as they were ventured at the time, not without some conviction of their justice, I am still ready to maintain them.

Pope was one of the first who gave praise to Akenside's chief work;[147] and perhaps his word conduced greatly to establish its reputation. Hammond's death happened two years before Pope's. Collins published his epistle to Sir T. Hanmer, and his Persian eclogues, some time before that event.[148] Miss Seward herself allows of Thomson's claim to a place in the Augustan aera, as it is sometimes called; and this being the case, Mallet's follows of course, since he frequently wrote in conjunction with that charming poet: Lyttelton[149] as well had the honour of being intimate with him. The name of Welsted[150] next occurs, which is mentioned by the Satirist in the following terms:

> Flow, Welsted, flow, like thine inspirer beer;
> Tho' stale, not ripe; tho' thin, yet never clear:
> So sweetly mawkish, and so smoothly dull,
> Heady, not strong, o'er flowing, tho' not full.

[*DunB* 5:3.169-72.]

Yet the person thus stigmatized is now beginning to obtain attention, and even respect. Miss S. however, thus expresses herself: "I did not chuse to bring forward, for the honour of Pope's period, any of the heroes of his inimitable Dunciad." Something like indignation arises on the perusal of this sentence. Will then the admirers of this allowedly great writer consent to sacrifice the fame of every one whom this splenetic and vindictive spirit has marked out as the object of ridicule or detestation? It may be hoped, that, on reflexion, so rash an opinion will be revoked. The fair critic does not think proper to notice the name of Garth,[151] though surely of some consideration, even from having gained the lavish praises of her favourite, yet, on this plea, Lord Lansdowne, Walsh, Wycherley, Trumball [sic],[152] and others, will obtain respectable seats in the poetic synod. Fenton and Broome assisted the translator of Homer in his version of the Odyssey; and executed their parts with such spirit, that they are scarcely to be distinguished from the pen of their master. This will be admitted as an undeniable claim.

It is the opinion of my respectable opponent, that Time, instead of stamping their real estimation on admired writers, has rather a contrary effect; and "induces the generality of readers to set a double value on every beauty, and to pass over defects with indulgence." As instances, she brings among Dryden's contemporaries Denham, Lee, Roscommon, and Waller; and, from the second division, Parnell, Gay, Addison, Watts, and the two Philipps.[153] This assertion is incontrovertibly just: but it must be remembered, that while antiquity puts more than their intrinsic price on the few writers she preserves, as great, or even a greater number of equal value, at first are overwhelmed by her in oblivion.

It is very probable, that if those selected from the first class "had lived, and produced their poems *now*, they would not have had many admirers." Yet this must not be attributed to any natural deficiency in their genius, but rather to the difference of tastes in the two ages. Had Lee been placed in the present times, he would have been obliged to discard his bombast, and might still have preserved his pathetic powers. Waller in the same case might have been prompted to despise the conceitedness of thought, which in his day was so much esteemed; and would have found that species of versification already perfect to his hand, which he spent so much labour in improving, while yet in its rude and unpolished infancy: and, by these means, Denham's verses would not have incurred the imputation of being in general "heavy, laboured, and inharmonious." So necessary is it to consider, not only the writers themselves, but the ages in which they existed. We now come to the comparative merits of our two poetic rivals. Every one knows, and laments, (let me again repeat) that Dryden, from the unfortunate and pressing state of his affairs, was frequently obliged to be hasty and negligent, and had not time to make selections from the multiplicity of images and expressions, which constantly crowded on his pen. For this reason I thought it hard and ungenerous that his most defective passages should be contrasted with the lively and polished graces of the younger Bard. As for the fear of "our young writers being tempted into a coarse and weedy style," there is not the shadow of a danger that Mr. Weston's sentiments on this subject will have so great a prevalence over the rising generation, which is more inclined to degenerate into the contrary extreme.

While Dryden, studying to render his poetic garden rather spacious than nicely beautiful, suffered the rankest weeds to spring up among the most luxuriant flowers, and entirely neglected the assistance of art; Pope, with deliberate leisure, was employed in banishing every appearance of disorder, in adjusting his delicate plants in the most striking dispositions, and in checking, sometimes too severely, the sportive wantonness of Nature. There are some, who (to preserve the metaphor) are on the whole more delighted with the wilderness of the former, than with the regular, yet elegant parterres of the latter; and I profess myself to be one of the number. I conclude with adding the testimonies of two deservedly celebrated modern poets in favour of Dryden. Gray, finishing one of his letters to Dr. Beattie, has these remarkable words, "Remember Dryden, and be blind to all his faults."[154] And Mr. Warton calls Palamon and Arcite "the most animated and harmonious piece of versification in the English language." History of English Poetry, chap. 23, p. 364.[155]

Yours, &c. M[arcellu]s.

---

* This and the following letters, received in October, were kept back till Mr. Weston had compleated his vindication. Edit.

12.

Mr. Urban,   *Oct.* 14. [1789]
["M.F." continues his argument with Weston over the names they have called each other.]

Mr. W. objects mostly to Mr. Pope's satirical pieces; their acrimony he thinks too severe on many worthy characters. This may in part be true; I think I have before acquiesced to it: but we ought to consider Mr. Pope's provocations, his abilities, and the swarm of minor Poets that were constantly nibbling at him; and "many with his provocations, and many with his abilities"[156] would, like him, have consigned them to everlasting fame.

I am yet to learn in what Pope "injured the poetical constitution," in what respect "he trampled on the rights of those citizens he ought to have loved and protected." I know nothing of this sort in Pope's history, nor that he had any "pretences to piety and morality" that were unreal; he must have been very artful and very wicked, to "impose on the understandings, and seduce the affections, of the rich and powerful;" though it must be acknowledged, that riches and power do not at a dead certainty produce wisdom and caution. Mr. Pope, it seems, was too hard for them, and made them his "stepping stones" to the highest seat on the Parnassian mount; for to that highest seat he certainly did attain. And shall he rest quietly in his grave for this? No; Mr. W. is determined to gibbet him *in terrorem*[157] to all future tyrants. Pardon me, my good Sir; but this too is like the Roman bigots, *manfully* attacking the "cerements"[158] of the venerable Wickliff, and wreaking their vengeance on his passive remains, after their peaceable interment forty years. Yours, &c. M. F.

13.

Mr. Urban,   *Oct.* 31. [1789]

["Impartial" begins by praising Miss Seward's *Louisa*, asserting that her "landscape painting" has not "been equalled by Dryden, nor surpassed by Milton."]

I agree with your elegant and ingenious, and, as far as one can judge from his writings, your upright and amiable correspondent, Mr. Weston, in giving up to the detestation of the considerate Pope's treatment of Leonard Welsted. And what shall we say to his satire on that profound scholar and virtuous man Dr. Samuel Clarke?[159] Had a writer of inferior abilities to Pope been guilty of such conduct, he would have been damned to everlasting infamy. And yet, great talents, instead of softening the harsh feature of vice, should only serve to make them appear the more deformed. Dryden may have flattered Guilt, but I do not know that he has degraded Excellence.   Yours, &c. Impartial.

14.

Mr. Urban,   *Solihull, April 25*. [1790]

[Weston says he intends now to give his proofs of "Pope's Baseness of Heart."]

96

Discarding, of Course, every idea of bringing forward Pope's *Meanness* to Broome, *Hypocrisy* to Hughes and Hill, *Treachery* to Bolingbroke, *Baseness* to Welsted, Lord Harvey [Hervey] and Lady Mary Wortley Montague, and *Ingratitude* to Chandos[160] and Addison — (Facts — the Truth of which has been disputed) — I determined to confine myself to one substantial Instance of his Villainy, which, standing recorded by Himself, should laugh to Scorn the very Possibility of Denial. — But the Subject unfortunately happened to be of a Nature so *peculiarly* horrible and disgusting, as to render a Discussion of it — in a Letter intended for the Perusal of a Lady — impossible.   Joseph Weston.

To M. F.   *Solihull, April* 25. [1790]
[Weston says this is "the last Notice" he intends to take of "M.F." He continues the wrangle over the names they have called each other.]
    But to the point in question.
    The following is extracted from an early Edition of the Dunciad, Book III.[161]

> "Behold yon Pair, in Strict Embraces join'd;
> How like in manners, and how like in mind!
> Fam'd for Good-Nature, Burnet, and for Truth;
> Ducket for Pious Passion to the Youth.
> Equal in Wit, and equally Polite,
> Shall this a Pasquin, that a Grumbler write;
> Like are their merits, like rewards they share,
> That shines a Consul, this Commissioner.   [5:3.173-80.]

REMARKS.

V.175. *Fam'd for good nature*, Burnet, &c.
Ducket *for pious passion to the youth*]
    The first of these was son of the late bishop of *S.* Author of a weekly Paper called *the Grumbler*, as the other was concerned in another called *Pasquin*, in which Mr. *Pope* was abused with the late Duke of *Buckingham* and Bishop of *Rochester*. They also joined in a piece against his first undertaking to translate the Iliad, intitled *Homerides*, by Sir *Iliad Dogrel*, printed 1715.[162] Mr. *Curll* gives us this further account of Mr. *Burnet*. "He did *himself write* a Letter to the E. of *Halifax, informing his Lordship* (as he tells him) *of what he knew much better before.* And he published *in his own name* several political pamphlets, A certain Information of a certain Discourse, a Second Tale of a Tub, &c. *All which* it is strongly afirmed *were written by* Colonel *Ducket.* Curll, *Key*, p. 17. But the author of the

Characters of the Times tells us, the political pieces were not approved of by his *own father*, the Reverend Bishop.

Of the other works of these Gentlemen, the world has heard no more than it would of Mr. *Pope's*, had their united laudable endeavours discouraged him from his undertaking. How few good works had ever appeared (since men of true merit are always the least presuming) had there been always such champions to stifle them in their conception? And were it not better for the Publick, that a million of monsters should come into the world, which are sure to die as soon as born, than that the Serpents should strangle one *Hercules* in his cradle?

The Union of these two Authors gave Occasion to this Epigram:

> Burnet and Ducket, friends in Spite,
>   Came hissing forth in verse;
> Both were so forward, each would write,
>   So Dull, each hung an a —
> Thus Amphisboena[163] (I have read)
>   At either end assails;
> None knows which leads, or which is led,
>   For both heads are but tails.   [5:3.175-76n.]

Here is a Charge of the most atrocious, the most unnatural, the most detestable Kind, brought against Colonel Ducket; for it is not possible for any one possessed of common Sense, and common Modesty, *to sign his name* to an Opinion that Pope meant *really* to praise Burnet for Good-nature and for Truth, or that he intended to celebrate the Wit or the Politeness of either Party. (The beastly Epigram settles that Point beyond all Controversy.) — The whole Passage is evidently *ironical*, and clearly calculated to impress the Reader with an Idea that both were the *Reverse* of Witty — both the *Reverse* of Polite; that Burnet was *famed* for Ill-nature and Falsehood; and that Ducket was *famed* for an *impious* Passion for the Youth. — It only remains to examine whether this horrid Accusation was well-founded or not.

In Consequence of the Colonel's spirited Conduct on this extraordinary Attack, Pope found it *convenient* to add the following Note.

'V. 167. [176] — for pious Passion to the Youth — The Verse is a literal Translation of Virgil, *Nisus amore pio pueri* — and here, as in the Original, applied to Friendship; that between Nisus and Euryalus is allowed to make one of the most amiable Episodes in the World, and *surely* never was interpreted in a *perverse* Sense. But it will *astonish* the *Reader* to *hear*, that on *no other* Occasion than *this Line*, a Dedication was written to this Gentleman to induce him to think *something further*. "Sir, you are known to have all that Affection for the beautiful Part of the Creation which God and Nature designed — Sir, you have a very fine Lady — and, Sir, you have eight very fine children" — &c. [Dedic. to Dennis Rem. on the Rape of the Lock.][164] The Truth is,the poor Dedicator's Brain was turned upon this Article; he had taken into his Head that ever since some Books were written against the *Stage*, and since the *Italian Opera* had prevailed, the Nation was infected with a Vice not fit to be named: He went so far as to print upon the Subject, and concludes his argument with this Remark, "that he cannot help thinking the Obscenity of Plays excusable at this Juncture; since, when that execrable Sin is spread so wide, it may be of Use to the reducing Men's Minds to the natural Desire of Women." Dennis, *Stage defended* against Mr. *Law*, p. 20.[165] Our Author Solemnly Declared, he never heard any Creature *but* the Dedicator mention That Vice and This Gentleman together.' [*DunA* 5:3.176n.]

What Power of Language can do Justice to the Sentiments of Indignation which this most impudent Attempt to impose on the Understanding excites? — However, the Acknowledgment in the last Line of this fallacious Note signs Pope's Passport to Everlasting Infamy. — Confessing that he had not even the smallest Ground for the Diabolical Charge, yet conscious that, while the most obnoxious Couplet remained, none but ideots *could* avoid seeing the Matter in its true Light, he, at last, thought it expedient to expunge it, and to alter the Notes in the following Manner.

"Behold yon Pair, &c.) *One* of these was Author of a weekly Paper called *The Grumbler*, as the other was concerned in another called *Pasquin*, in which Mr. *Pope* was abused with the Duke of Buckingham, and Bishop of *Rochester*. They also joined in a Piece against his first undertaking to translate the *Iliad*, intituled *Homerides*, by *Sir Iliad Doggrel*, printed 1715." (Eleven succeeding Lines are omitted.) "Of the other Works of their Gentlemen, &c." — (to the End of the Paragraph.)

"The Union of these two Authors gave Occasion to this Epigram:
" — — — and Ducket, friends in Spite, &c." (to the End of the Epigram).

"After many Editions of this Poem, the Author thought fit to omit the Names of *these two Persons*, whose Injury to him was of so old a Date. In the Verses he omitted, it was said that *one* of them had a *pious Passion* for the *other*. It was a literal Translation of Virgil, &c." [*DunB* 5:3.179n.]

Mark, gentle Reader, the curious Reason *intimated* for the *Omission* of *both* Names in the Poem, while *one* of them is retained in the Note! — But Ducket was probably dead, and Burnet was probably become a judge![166]

And now, Mr. M. F. I take a final Leave!

If, after this unembellished Statement of facts, you *can* believe that Pope did *not* attempt to fix this most loathsome and most horrible Stigma on an innocent Man — or, being convinced that he *did* attempt it, *can* believe him to be less than a Villain — you are welcome to *think* Me as vile a Slanderer, and as consummate a Scoundrel, as I have *proved* Him to be! Joseph Weston.

15.

Lichfield Close.   *June 16.* [1790]

Once for all, Mr. Urban, permit me to observe, that Mr. Weston's original charge against Pope remains wholly unsupported. In the controverted Preface to the Woodmen of Arden, its Author professes to have found "amusement, alloyed with indignation, in tracing the insidious arts which Pope suffered his friends to practise to undermine the fame of Dryden, and exalt himself into the vacant chair."[167]

Mr. Weston has been repeatedly called upon to exhibit *some* of these numerous proofs. He closes the controversy without producing one of them. It is plain, therefore, that those proofs had only an imaginary existence in the strange violence of his prejudices; and Pope stands clear of the imputed meanness; for it is contrary to all justice, when a person is arraigned of one crime, to condemn him upon evidence of another, which is perfectly dissimilar.

That Pope, when incensed, was often vindictive to a faulty extreme, has never been denied; but what has his conduct to an absurd fellow, who had abused him, to do with the imputed treachery to *Dryden?* How does *that* prove him the artful source of those numerous critical decisions, which pronounced Pope the brilliant reformer of Dryden's vulgarities, and slovenly versification?

Mr. Weston once read to me an abusive poem of Welsted's upon Pope.[168] It was by no means ill-written; but it attempted to deprive the latter of every pretension to genius and worth. Mr. Weston acknowledged that this Philippic passed the press before the Dunciad, and the priority acquits Pope of every thing like *baseness* to Welsted. Where is the baseness of retorting the charge of poetic inability in lines whose wit and spirit prove the injustice of the *first* accuser?

In [GM] p. 386,[169] my antagonist challenges me to produce that confutation of his arguments in his letter, [GM] p. 27,[170] to which I have said they are given. Thus then — he triumphantly quotes the original in vindication of that vulgar harangue which Dryden has made for the Empress of Heaven.

> "When labouring still with endless discontent,
> The Queen of Heaven did thus her fury *vent*:
> Then am I vanquish'd, must I yield, *said she*,
> And must the Trojans reign in Italy?
> So Fate will have it, and Jove adds his force,
> Nor can my power divert their *happy* course.
> Shall [Cou'd] angry Pallas, with revengeful spleen,
> The Grecian navy *burn*, and *drown* the *men*?
> Shall [She]," &c. [*Ae* 4:1.54-62.]

The original writer is certainly responsible for the sentiments and imagery; but for the manner in which they are expressed in another language the translator *solely*. We all know that vulgar expressions may convey the *sense* of a foreign author, though that sense may have been primarily given in words that have no congenial meanness. If Mr. Weston does *not feel* the verbal bathos of the "*said she*" in the third line, and the "burn the navy" — "drown the men," in the *last*, his insensibility gives proof that poetic genius and poetic taste may be disunited. How easy to express Virgil's sense as faithfully with less inelegance!

> When, with the dark'ning frown of angry pride,
> In haughty tone, imperial Juno cried:
> Then am I vanquish'd, shall the Trojans gain.
> Triumphant empire on the Latian plain?
> While gods and men my powerless efforts see,
> Jove and the Fates this hated doom decree.
> Shall injur'd Pallas, with avenging aim,
> O'erwhelm the Greeks, and wrap their fleets in flame?
> Shall she, &c.

If the above lines equally express Virgil's meaning, without the ludicrous inelegance that disgrace Dryden's, Mr. Weston's *first* argument is confuted.

His other pleas, which seek to prove the certainty that Dryden was *not* the translator of the Epistle from Helen to Paris, though he avows it *solely* his through all the editions, are set aside by those passages, of *equal* inelegance, which have been already cited in the course of this controversy, from the Hind and Panther, Ode on the Death of Anne Killigrew, the Virgil,[171] and other of his works. Upon most of those quotations Mr. Weston wisely makes *no* comment, willing, doubtless, that his readers should forget them, being utterly destructive of his unfor[t]unate assertion, that the style of the great Dryden is never *injudiciously* debased. My edition of Dryden's Works contains no *second* version of Dido to Aeneas; and the first, from which Mr. Weston quotes, and calls *charming*,[172] appears to me a collection of vapid, stiff, inharmonious lines, interspersed with a few beautiful couplets, but all along disgraced with such writing as the following, that certainly challenges the worst lines in the Helen to Paris, and *resembles* them sufficiently to leave no doubt, with the unprejudiced, that their origin is the *same.*

> "Built walls you shun, unbuilt you seek; that land
> Is yet to conquer, but you this command.
> Suppose you landed where your wish design'd,
> Think what reception foreigners would find.
> When will your towers the height of Carthage know?
> Or when your eyes discern such crowds below?
> If such a town and subjects you could see,
> Still would you want a wife that [who] lov'd like me."
> [*DA* 1:13-16, 21-24.]

Lord Mulgrave could not jingle couplets that less deserved the name of Poetry; nor is the general style of this Epistle, which Mr. Weston calls *charming*, a whit more elevated.

His quotation from Warton[173] perfectly meets my sentiments; the most simple and common expressions are frequently beautiful when they harmonize with the general style, and suit the character of the speaker. When they do *not*, prosaic flatness, or ridiculous vulgarity, results from their use. The words *burn, drown, men*, sound ludicrous as they are applied and combined by the imperial Juno; yet the two first, from being used in a metaphoric sense, and the last from different combination, are capable of acquiring great dignity; instance, Galatea on the Sea: vide that celebrated poem *The Botanic Garden.*

> "And as the lustre of her eye she turns,
> Soft sighs the gale, and amorous Ocean *burns.*"[174]

Also Pope:

> "As the rapt Seraph that adores and *burns.*"
> [*EOM* 3.1:1:278.]

And so the word *drown* in Hayley's beautiful Ode on Howard:

> "See that [yon] sweet rustic *drown'd* in tears."[175]

And the word *men*, in Pope's Homer:

"To gods and men to give the golden day." [*Od* 9:3.4]

If it is felt, from these examples, that the *same* words, according to their sense and combinations, may be vulgarly prosaic, or beautifully poetic, then it remains evident, that Mr. Weston's observation was not meant to justify Dryden's style, when it sunk so *low* as in passages frequently quoted in my letters upon this subject. I question not its having, in many places, acquired *beauty* from the use of those common expressions, that very often were so *applied* as to *disgrace* it.

And now, having produced that confutation of Mr. Weston's arguments in his former letter, which his latter challenged, I resolve never more to resume the subject; glad that no proofs can be brought of meanness used to acquire fame, which, in so great a writer as Pope, appeared utterly improbable. I confess it were to be wished that his disposition had been as free from acrimony as his verse from imperfection: nor need such exemption to have robbed the world of the inimitable Dunciad, since the *generality* of the corrections inflicted there are no more incompatible with sweetness of temper, than the prosecuting a thief who has robbed, or a ruffian who has assaulted us.

If with a single being, *but* Mr. Weston, it can *yet* remain a doubt, whether Dryden's style of versification in the heroic couplet, or Pope's, be the most happy, let him compare *Dryden's* Translation of the first book of Homer's Iliad and *Pope's*. He will find the latter conveying, with brilliant strength and harmonious sweetness, the same sense in a *less* number of lines than Dryden, with his feeble Alexandrines in the middle of sentences, and botching triplets; the superior conciseness is in a proportion of about eight to twelve. Anna Seward.

16.

Mr. Urban, *Jan. 15.* [1790]

Your known impartiality gives me to hope you will admit a few more observations on Mr. Weston's defence, and in vindication of Mr. Pope; whom Mr. W. intends to make the great witness of his own *infamous delinquency*, and to convince us that he was an "execrable impostor,"[176] "a foe to human-kind."[177]

* * * *

No less a man than Lord Orrery has asserted, "that this 'foe to human-kind, this execrable Pope,' treated his friends with a politeness that charmed, and a generosity that was much to his honour; every guest was made happy within his doors; pleasure dwelt under his roof, and elegance presided at his table."[178] Lord Orrery knew the man; he would not hazard such an eulogium at random, and without due conviction of its justice.

The excellent Addison, or at least a literary associate, with his approbation, introduces that divine poem the Messiah, in the Spectator, with the following terms: "I will make no apology for entertaining the reader with the following poem, which is written by *a great genius, a friend of mine* in the country, who is not ashamed to employ his wit in the praise of his Maker."[179] Yet this *friend* of Addison's, who thus praiseth his Maker, is Mr. Weston's "*execrable impostor*," his "*foe to human-kind*!"

It would be no difficult task to adduce testimonies in favour of Mr. Pope from many of the greatest names of the last age. Arbuthnot, Atterbury, Swift, Steele, Gay, and many others, might be brought. But why mention what is so well-known to all literary men? It would be occupying your valuable work unnecessarily. Mr. Weston's *ipse dixit*, like a torrent, is to bear down all before it. These men were nothing more than *simple dupes* to Mr. Pope's artful duplicity and cunning; like Satan he beguiled them; and they were foolish enough to esteem him an agreeable companion, an elegant poet, and a very desirable friend.

I felt no "exultation"[180] in asking Mr. W. whether he would have attacked Mr. Pope, had they been contemporaries. I asked a simple question, and he has answered it. He will, I hope, excuse me if I have my doubts. I have known men talk of wonderful prowess when danger has irreturnably passed by; whose "courage would have ouzed out at every pore"[181] under the idea of immediate contest.

["M.F." concludes by resuming the wrangle over name-calling.]†

M. F.

---

† Mr. Weston's final Answer to Miss Seward, from its extraordinary length, and from its not arriving more early in the month, is unavoidably postponed to our next.

17.

Mr. Urban, *Feb. 8.* [1790]

With satisfaction I read Mr. Morfitt's letter in your January Magazine.[182] We might reasonably expect his interference in the interesting dispute between Miss Seward and Mr. Weston. He has interfered, and that in a manly and candid sort, in a manner that evinces him equally learned and ingenuous. I trust, from his mode of writing, he will not deem me his adversary, though I may happen somewhat to differ from him.

Notwithstanding Mr. Morfitt prefers the poetry of Dryden to that of his successor, Pope, he does not acrimoniously deem the latter *execrable*, but touches on the moral character of each with a gentle hand, and kindly pleads in excuse for both. In his opinion, Mr. Dryden was a greater, and yet a less, poet than Mr. Pope; greater in his sublime flights, lesser in his depressive flats: and I believe his opinion is founded on justice, and accurate discrimination. — Mr. Pope's verses, though beautiful and excellent, he thinks tiresome, from their uniformity, and he "pants for hill and dale." Certainly contrast and variety are as necessary to relieve the "mind's eye" as that of the body. With him and Mr. Weston I agree, that an uniform, mellifluous flow of the finest verse wearies the attention, and unavoidably brings on satiety. Nature exhibits an inexhaustible variety in all around us; we have light and darkness, good and evil, pleasure and pain, and a thousand other contrasts; of which we constantly experience the necessary alternation, and without which, in our present state, we should undoubtedly be miserable, for we live but by change.

Mr. Morfitt complains of his satiety by the time he has read 200 pages of Mr. Pope; but I cannot consider this as decisive against the excellence of the poetry: that it evidences the frailty of the human intellect, most certainly must be allowed, and demonstrates our inability to bear a long succession of beautiful ideas without approaching fatigue. Sure I am, I never could read 200 pages of *any author, on any subject, poetry or prose*, without a desire of relieving the attention by a walk, or business of some kind. Undoubtedly, the modern mode of printing poetry, especially in our three-shilling and half-crown quartos, much favour one's getting through a good number of pages at a sitting; for

> Deep margins, large letters, and lines at a distance,
> Stead of Genius prolific, become their assistance:[183]

and, by-the-bye, Mr. Urban, they seem more calculated to attack the pocket than to improve the head, or amend the heart.

I cannot altogether agree with Mr. Weston, or Mr. Morfitt, that Mr. Pope's poetry is so uniformly destitute of the sublimer flights; nor can it plead a total exemption from the "depressive flats" which these gentlemen think so essentially necessary to constitute genuine poetry. No one appeared more sensible of this necessary variety than Mr. Pope himself; witness his letter to *one Walsh*, July 2, 1706, where he says, "I am convinced, as well as you, that one may correct too much; for in poetry, as in painting, a man may lay colours, one upon another, till they stiffen and deaden the piece. Besides, to bestow heightening on every part is monstrous. Some parts ought to be lower than the rest; and nothing looks more ridiculous than a work where the thoughts, however different in their own nature, seem all on a level. It is like a meadow newly mown, where weeds, grass, and flowers are all laid even, and appear undistinguished. I believe too, that sometimes our first thoughts are the best, as the first squeezing of the grapes makes the finest wine." Memoirs of A. Pope, by Wm. Ayre, Esq. 1745, 12 mo. [sic] p. 25.[184]

A poet, who thus expresses himself in a letter to his friend, I can never think would be so totally unmindful of his own declared sentiments as directly to give into that extreme and never-varying uniformity he had so justly and so properly condemned.

One might suppose this identical *one Walsh* was just now announced to the world by Mr. Weston, who, from his deeper researches into poetical anecdote, had made the discovery of Pope's poetical adviser to correctness; yet this *one Walsh*, this literary non-descript, is well known to have been a gentleman of considerable merit and consequence, author of several esteemed pieces in prose and verse, and, in the opinion of Mr. Weston's favourite Bard, even Dryden himself (in his Postscript to Virgil), the best critick of our nation in his time.[185] That he was high in the estimation of Mr. Pope is clear from the following lines:

> ——"Walsh, the Muse's judge and friend,
> Who justly knew to blame or to commend;
> To failings mild, but zealous for desert,
> The clearest head, and the sincerest heart,
> This humble praise, lamented shade, receive,
> This praise at least a grateful Muse may give.
> The Muse whose early voice you taught to sing,
> Prescrib'd her heights, and prun'd her tender wing,
> (Her guide now lost) no more attempts to rise,
> But in low numbers short excursions tries." [*EOC* 1:729-38.]

Yours, &c. M. F.

18.

Mr. Urban, *Solihull, Sept.* 25. [1790]

[Weston asserts Miss Seward has claimed victory and retired before the war is over.]

Permit me, therefore, Mr. Urban, to *justify* the Motives which influenced me in my Attack upon Pope's moral Character; and account for my Detestation of his Principles and Conduct.

Miss Seward *supposes* that the Dunciad was written in Consequence of Insults and Injuries received by him from the Individuals whom he stigmatizes as Knaves and Fools. Such once was *my* Opinion; but, on examining the Preface, Advertisement, Notes, Testimonies of Authors, &c. more closely, I found so much Reason to suspect the Truth of the Assertions, and the Fidelity of the Quotations, that I employed much Time, and no small Assiduity, in procuring the Works of these same Knaves and Fools: and the Result was — a Total Conviction of the Baseness and Malignity of the Duncifier's Disposition. By far the greater Part of the supposed Delinquents (as I remarked in a former Letter)[186] had given him *no* reasonable Cause for Resentment, and the intended Punishment of the Remainder immeasurably exceeded the Offence.

I plainly discovered that many a *disingenuous* — nay, many a Villainous Artifice was brought into Play — to degrade the Abilities, and blacken the Characters, not only of those who had spoken, or written, slightingly of himself or his Works, but also of those who had *not*; and his Treatment of whom must, therefore, arise from other Causes than those which he thought proper to assign: partly, perhaps, from Envy or Jealousy of those Talents which, if not timely crushed, might one Day rival his own — and partly, perhaps, from a parasitical Desire to please such of his Friends as had been animadverted upon by the Writers whom he affects to hold in Contempt.

But, whatever might be his Inducement, his Conduct I found to be such as inspired me with Horror and Indignation; and I fancied that I should render an essential Service to the Cause of Virtue and Humanity, by exposing the Hypocrisy of his Pretences and the Villainy of his Practices. — Full of this Idea, I constructed a Poem, a large Portion of which I appropriated to the Vindication of those whom he has so grossly traduced in that wicked Libel which my amiable but misguided Friend calls the "inimitable Dunciad;"[187] — intending to publish it with Notes and Illustrations. — But, when the first Ebullitions of Resentment had subsided, and I came coolly to meditate on the Magnitude of the Undertaking, and its probable Consequences, my Ardour for Publication was somewhat abated.... they who were obliged to own that Pope *was* a bad Man might wonder, or *affect* to wonder, what good Purpose could be answered by *proving* him one.

I was staggered by these and similar Reflections; and I let year after Year pass away, without coming to any Resolution. — At length Dr. Johnson's Lives of the Poets appeared; and you may guess, Mr. Urban, my Surprize and Pleasure at finding his Sentiments of Pope's Disposition in so many respects coincide with mine![188] — But, attentively as he

107

had studied the Poet's Character, I had studied it yet *more* attentively; and will frankly own that I felt no small Gratification in the Consciousness of having anticipated almost all his Observations, and of having made many others which had escaped even *his* scrutinizing Vigilance.

[Weston repeats his charges against Pope's character. He enlarges on his correction of Miss Seward's "Misconstruction" of accusation against Pope. In his *Preface to the Woodmen of Arden*, he wrote that Pope " 'suffered' " (not "incited," as Miss Seward misquoted him) " 'his *Friends* to practice (insidious arts) in order to undermine the Reputation of the deceased Poet (Dryden)."]

To prove that Pope really *did* suffer his Friends to depreciate the Person from whom he learned *all that is valuable* in the Structure of his Verse were a very easy Task indeed. — To mention only One (but that one an Host!) — Miss Seward cannot forget Swift — the Partner of Pope's Labours and the Friend of his Bosom; — Nor can she forget his Comparison of Dryden's Virgil to a Mouse under a Canopy of State:[189] no — nor his grave assertion in his Dedication of his Tale of a Tub to a Prince Posterity:

> "I do affirm, upon the Word of a sincere Man, that there is now actually in Being a certain Poet, called John Dryden, whose Translation of Virgil was lately printed in a large Folio, well-bound, and, if diligent Search were made, for aught I know, is yet to be seen."[190]   (*To be continued.*)

19.

Mr. Urban,   *June* 15. [1790]

Mr. Weston has taken his final leave of me somewhat in dudgeon; although he says he is in tolerable good-humour, from his manner I cannot but have my doubts. By addressing his last letter particularly to me, he in some measure demands of me a reply. His last arrow is now shot against Mr. Pope; by an unnatural exertion he has drawn his bow to its utmost stretch, overshot his mark, but the object of his wrath remains unhurt.

What has Mr. W. told us more than every one acquainted with Mr. Pope's writings knew before; the whole is extracted from the notes to the Dunciad, save a few egregiously perverse comments, similar to those of his predecessor John Dennis. It is not possible to confute this tale of slander better than Mr. Pope's own notes confute it.

It is acknowledged on all hands, that Mr. Pope was previously abused by Burnet and Duckett.[191] Mark, reader, they threw the first stone. Aye;

but then Pope ought to have been passively obedient, perfectly non-resistent: how presumptuous to defend himself! how execrable to retort! The abuse it seems was from the firm of Ducket and Co.; they wrote Homerides, Grumblers, Pasquins, &c. It was a sort of amphisboena abuse; and the satiric retort properly included them both:

"Behold yon pair in strict embraces join'd,
How like in manners, and how like in mind!
Fam'd for good-nature, Burnet, and for truth;
Ducket for pious passion to the youth.
Equal in wit, and equally polite,
Shall this a Pasquin, that a Grumbler write.
Like are their merits, like rewards they share,
That shines a Consul, this Commissioner."

[*DunA* 3:3.173-80.]

The redoubtable John Dennis took it into his head to annex such an idea to the fourth line (though a literal translation from a Latin classick) as no one else had thought of, and particularly pointed it out to the gentleman concerned, who, it is wonderful, never discovered that meaning himself, if that was the real intent of the satire. What was the Colonel's "spirited conduct"[192] on this trying calumny? No doubt the laws of his country would award him excessive damages on so just an occasion: had he recourse to this mode? if not, had he recourse to any? What man alive could be passive under such obloquy?

I always take it for granted an author knows his own meaning at least as well as any of his readers; and Mr. Pope having solemnly declared he had never heard any such detestable report coupled with Mr. Ducket's name, or that any such idea guided him when he penned the obnoxious lines, what right had Dennis, or any of his successors, to point out to Mr. Ducket, or to posterity, a meaning which the author totally disavows, and has used every endeavour to do away? It is certain, if the matter was as pointed out by Dennis and Mr. Weston, of loading an innocent man with such a vile accusation, the attempt was a most villainous one, and deserving the severest censure. But, on his supposition, what possible motive can be alledged for Mr. Pope's conduct in this matter? He must know that the accusation would immediately confute itself, seeing no one had ever thought or surmized any such thing, nor was there any possibility of such a non-entity charge ever being made good, consequently the ridiculousness and baseness of it must effectualy secure him from making it; hence I conclude that, in this matter, he is accused wrongfully.

Mr. Pope finding that Dennis's perverse comment was certain to be espoused by all his (Mr. Pope's) enemies (and his enviable talents had made them numerous), and perhaps, on their authority, taken up by others, thought proper, in later editions of the Dunciad, to expunge the obnoxious lines, as the best reparation he could make the injured party; injured by Dennis greatly more than by himself, whom though he intended to lash for his prior abuse, he could not mean to cast on him the most odious stigma possible to be cast on man; a stigma which, as he had never heard surmized by any one, it is next to impossible he should ever think of applying.

Mr. W, in his Poetical Address to Miss Seward, has termed Mr. Pope "a weaver of mechanic verse."[193] We may safely assert, that few poetical looms have produced such exquisite work; the fineness of the tissue, the delicacy and durability of the materials, have been rarely equalled.

I shall now also take my final leave of this subject, and Mr. W; yet in perfect good-will and good-humour, highly respecting his talents as a poet, a man of learning, and a gentleman, and wishing to forget his prejudices. If he is disposed to add "more last words,"[194] he will meet with no interruption or reply from me, and may enjoy the great satisfaction of concluding the dispute. I shall continue to be of opinion, notwithstanding all that has been alledged, from John Dennis even to Joseph Weston, that the poetry of Mr. Pope will continue to be read and admired when the comments of his enemies are forgotten, or remembered but through the medium of his celebrity.   Yours, &c. M. F.

20.

To M. F.

Sir,   *Solihull, Oct.* 11. [1790]

[Weston justifies himself in again replying to "M.F."]

The *chief* Source of your Incredulity with Respect to the horrible Tendency of the Lines which you have quoted from the Dunciad seems to be — the implicit Confidence you repose in Pope's Veracity; but that Confidence will be shaken to its Foundation when in the Magazine for next November,[195] you shall find Proofs on Proofs that he was in the Habit of slandering Reputations, and afterwards denying, or explaining away, his manifest Intention: then — feeling rather shocked than convinced by his "solemn Declarations" — you will perceive that it Was possible for him to attempt the Ruin of a Character, by an atrocious Artifice — and, on being threatened with personal Chastisement, that it was Also possible for him to sneak behind a vile Subterfuge. Indeed, if "solemn Declarations" were to be considered as tantamount to Exculpation, Tyburn and Botany Bay would frequently have Reason to complain that they were defrauded of their Due.

* * * *

I never asserted — I never *meant* to assert — that Pope ought to have been "passively obedient, perfectly non-resistant," when his poetical Reputation was assailed; I did not blame him for retaliating: it was only his Mode of Retaliation which I condemned. If Burnet and Ducket Did "throw the *first Stone*,"[196] was a *Stab in the Dark* a justifiable Retort? Is an unjust Censure of one Man's Talents to be returned by a more unjust Censure of another Man's Morals?

* * * *

You are *compelled* to grant — that Pope was Serious in his Praise of Ducket's Attachment to Burnet — or — that he was Not serious; that the Words "pious Passion" must mean Pure and Virtuous Friendship — or must mean Gross and Vicious Inclination: in fine, that he intended to ascribe to Ducket a Virtue which exalts Human Nature almost to angelic Excellence — or a vice which degrades it below Brutality. To ascertain in Which of these Senses the Words in Debate ought to be understood, I shall consider Two Points; either of which would *singly* decide the Dispute.

In the first Place, what was Pope's Design when he constructed the Dunciad?

Miss Seward shall answer the Question,

"To make his Enemies Ridiculous to all Ages."[197] And How was this charitable Purpose to be obtained? Could the Man who, by laughing In Print at his *intended* Translation of the Iliad,[198] attempted to injure him in Fame and in Fortune (and whom Pope could not, therefore, be violently disposed to *compliment*) — could this Man, I say, be made ridiculous to all *succeeding* Ages, by attributing to him a Virtue which had been celebrated with enthusiastic Ardour by the Poets, Philosophers, Orators, and Historians, of all *former* ones? a Virtue — sanctioned by a bright Example, to which all Christians ought to look up with reverential Awe? — Impossible!

Shew me, Sir, a single Line in the Dunciad — shew me a single Line in the "Prose Rubbish"[199] which *encrusts* it — in which a Virtue, or the Shadow of a Virtue, is *seriously* imputed to Any of its Heroes!

On this solid Basis, Sir, I might *rest* my Argument, and bid Defiance to Confutation; but, rather than leave a *Scantling* of a Doubt on any Mind which Can be enlightened, I will take the superfluous Pains of con-

111

sidering the Connexion of the questionable Line with *that* which Precedes, and with *that* which Follows it.

> "Behold yon Pair, in Strict Embraces join'd;
> How like in Manners, and how like in Mind!
> *Fam'd* for Good-Nature, *Burnet*, and for Truth;
> *Ducket* for Pious Passion to the *Youth*.
> Equal in Wit, and equally Polite —"[200]

To prove the Praise in the *third* and *fifth* Lines to be Ironical — is to prove *that* in the *fourth* Line to be Also ironical; unless a single Passage in some Author — antient or modern — can be produced, in which one Line of Serious Praise is guarded, like a Deserter, before and behind, by two Lines of Mock Panegyrick!

If you *could*, sir, be so absurd as to believe that Pope, smarting from the Perusal of "Homerides," meant to extol Burnet, *in Earnest*, for Good-Nature, the auxiliary Epigram would instantly *confute* your Absurdity. Are not the Colleagues *there* expressly termed "Friends in Spite?" Are they not *there* expressly stigmatised for Dulness — in direct Opposition to the Verse which celebrates their Wit? How are these apparent Inconsistencies to be accounted for?

I, Sir, as well as You, "take it for granted that an Author knows his own Meaning at least as well as any of his Readers;" but I do Not take it for granted that he can mean Good and Evil *at the same Instant*. Pope could Not mean that his Enemies could be *at once* Good-Natured and Spiteful — *at once* Witty and Dull! He did know his own Meaning; he Well knew it: and was willing that his Readers should *likewise* know it. But he was treading on tender Ground, and Caution was requisite. Therefore, to gratify present Resentment, without making future Inconvenience, he wrapped that Meaning in oracular Ambiguity — in the Text; and, to rectify any Mistake which *inattentive* Readers might fall into by supposing him *serious* in his Praises, he added an *epigrammatic Commentary*, which sufficiently developed his Intention; and, by contradicting that Part of his Elogium which he Durst, instructed those Readers to contradict *for themselves* that Part which *he* durst Not.

This Supposition removes every Difficulty; the seeming Incongruity vanishes; the Text and Commentary are reconciled (irreconcileable on any *other* Principle): and his Conduct is clear and consistent.

Since then you must allow, of Force, the *third* and *fifth* Lines to be demonstrably Ironical — reflect, Sir, how much out of Place — out of Time — out of Character — would the *fourth* Line appear, if designed to be understood *literally* as attributing one of the most exalted Qualities which can ennoble the human Mind to a Man whom he was aiming "to make ridiculous to all Ages!"

The Absurdity is so palpably Gross, and the Inference so inevitably Conclusive, that I should deem it an Insult to *yourself*, Sir, as well as to a large Majority of Mr. Urban's Readers, to offer another Syllable on the Subject.

[Weston parts company with "M.F." urging forgiveness and good humour on both sides.]

Joseph Weston.

---

21. (continues Letter 20)
Mr. Urban,   *Solihull, Oct.* 11. [1790]

* * * *

I left off, if you recollect, with a Quotation from Swift, expressive of the utmost Contempt for Dryden's Translation of Virgil.[201] But how (Miss Seward may ask) can Pope be to blame? — Could He prevent Swift's Attack on Dryden any more than She could prevent mine on Pope? — Probably not; but He might have acted on that Occasion as she has on one nearly similar — *viz.* have called *his* Friend to a public Account for his "Prejudice" and "Want of Taste"[202] — My generous Assailant must surely allow that either She has done *too much* or he — *too little*!

[Addressing Miss Seward, Weston repeats his charges against Pope's character. He continues by correcting Miss Seward's quotations from Dryden.]

In your Magazine for May, 1789 (p. 390),[203] Miss Seward selects a Passage of uncommon Celebrity from Pope's Iliad, and compares it with one from the first and least meritorious of all Dryden's Productions — a Poem on the Death of Lord Hastings; a Piece which I believe is not inserted in *many* Editions of his Works: and, lest this inelegant Extract should not appear to *sufficient* Disadvantage, she flanks it by *another* celebrated Passage from Pope. Two against one, you know, Mr. Urban, are odds!

Her Management of the next Example she produces is still *less* advantageous to poor Dryden.[204] Extracting six Lines from Juno's Soliloquy, in the first Book of the Eneid (which she considers as unpoetical), she misquotes the Beginning of the Seventh, and skips over that and the four succeeding Lines (which are admirable), fastens on one which she thinks laughable, and omits the remaining Eight, which are excellent. I thought it but Justice to insert the *entire* Speech, accompanied by the Original, in your Miscellany for January, 1790.[205] Miss

113

Seward seems to consider this as a silent Rebuke, from the Manner in which she mentions my Quotation ([*GM*] p. 523) — "He *triumphantly* quotes the Original in Vindication of that *vulgar Harangue* which Dryden has made for the Empress of Heaven."[206]

Adverting a second Time to Juno's Soliloquy, a second Time she stops short at the seventh Line. But, to make Amends for the Omission of the Rest of this reprobated Speech, she has pressed into her Service the introductory Couplet, which contains the word "vent" — to which (by her Italicks) she seems to attach the idea of Flatness. She appears to have conceived an unaccountable Dislike to the Verbs "vent" — "burn" — and "drown" — unless used in a figurative sense; but, surely, they seem just as musical as "yield — "reign" — "add" — (which escape uncensured) — or any other Monosyllable Verbs! — The Substantive "Men" seems also to have fallen under her Displeasure; — but *why* — is not easy to discover. That it *may* be so applied or combined as to appear in a ludicrous light is true; — in the Mouth of a Coquet (for Instance), who declares "she is teazed to Death by these *odious* — Men"[207] it is ridiculous enough. But I cannot grant that it sounds *in*elegant when opposed to "*Ships*" — although it may be *more* elegant when opposed to "Gods."

On Miss Seward's Substitution of the metaphorical Phrase of "wrapping Fleets in Flame" — for "burning" them — I shall only remark that Dr. Harwood, disapproving of the beautiful Simplicity of "Jesus wept," altered it, in his Translation of the New Testament, to "Jesus burst into a Flood of Tears."[208] They who think *his* Amplification an Amendment will, of Course, be pleased with Miss Seward's.

Having sufficiently decried Dryden's Translation, she introduces her own, by exclaiming, "How easy to express Virgil's *Sense* as *faithfully* with less *Inelegance!*"[209] And, after heightening every Line of the contested Passage into splendid Versification, she adds, "If the above Lines *equally* express Virgil's *Meaning*, without the ludicrous Inelegance that disgraces Dryden's, Mr. Weston's *first* Argument is confuted."

Firm as Atlas stands my first Argument — for any Shock which her Translation gives it. "If the above Lines equally express Virgil's Meaning?" — But the above Lines unfortunately do Not equally express Virgil's Meaning! And (which is still more unfortunate) the only Resemblance which the first Couplet bears to the Original is couched in two Words — "when" in the first Line, and "Juno" in the second.

To the Proof.

> Cum Juno aeternum servans sub pectore vulnus
> Haec secum:[210]

114

Dryden.
"When labouring *still* with Endless Discontent,
The Queen of Heaven did thus her Fury vent."

Miss Seward.
"When, with the dark'ning Frown of angry Pride,
In haughty Tone, imperial Juno cried."

The Reader of true Taste may possibly deem the brilliant Additions of "dark'ning Frown" — — "angry Pride" and "haughty Tone" — an inadequate Recompence for the Loss of the much more important Information — that an insatiable Desire of Revenge *unceasingly* rankled in Juno's Breast. Virgil evidently refers to the "saevae memorem Junonis ob iram" in the Opening of the Eneid;[211] a Circumstance on which the Machinery of the Poem *hinges*: and, therefore, not to be omitted without manifest Detriment to the Poet's Plan. Besides — the Mantuan Bard was much too *judicious* to say All that he *could* have said on the Occasion; and paid his Reader's Imagination the Compliment of supposing that it would easily collect — from her Words — the *tone* and that which accompanied them.

But, were Miss Seward's Translation as faithful as it is erroneous, I should still remain unconfuted. I must beg leave once more, Mr. Urban, to remind your Readers of the principal Object of our Contention. I had expressed an Opinion that the Style of Dryden is preferable to that of Pope — On Account of the Inequalities which so frequently occur. How does my ingenious Opponent endeavour to overthrow that Opinion? Why truly, by proving that there Are those Inequalities! A Mode of Confutation entirely *new* — and not a little *comical*!

But stay! — Miss Seward will allow Poetic Diction to Sink — but not Too low. Now we come to the Point. Who is to be the Judge of the Precise Degree to which it may be allowed to descend? — Ah, Mr. Urban! Who indeed? — Until that question *be* answered, Miss Seward and I may argue for ever, without being one Jot nearer the Mark; for I cannot allow that *calling* Dryden's Translation a vulgar Harangue is *proving* it to be one; — any more than I can acknowledge the Justice of those severe Epithets with which she so plentifully besprinkles most of the Passages which she has judged it expedient to select.

As Dryden has contrived it, Juno pours out the Effusions of her Wrath in a regular Climax. One *sees* the offended Goddess working herself into a Passion by very natural Gradations. But Miss Seward has begun in so lofty a Strain, that I have litle Doubt of the Effect which would have been produced had she translated the *whole* Soliloquy!

115

The chief Blemish in *modern* poetic Diction is Inflation. If that Blemish is undiscoverable in Miss Seward's Works, it is probably owing to the Grandeur and Sublimity of her Conceptions; which *justify* the uniform Majesty of her Style. The *Shortness* of her Poems is a Circumstance also much in her Favour; for Pope's Version of the Iliad proves to every *unprejudiced* Judge, that unvaried Sweetness and unvaried Loftiness *will* tire — in a Work of any considerable Length. An Elegy and an Epic Poem demand very different Degrees of Polish.

So much for Miss Seward's boasted Confutation of my first Position!

In your Miscellany for May, 1789, p. 391, she has made some Extracts from Ovid's Epistle from Helen to Paris.[212] She did not chuse to quote from Canace to Macareus — nor from Dido to Eneas — but pitched upon the very worst of the three. Culling with uncommon Care the dullest Parts, she has made Stupidity appear *more* stupid, by tacking together Passages that were never intended to be joined, and which derive no small Inconvenience from the Union.

After quoting Two Lines, she omits Ten, then quotes Eighteen more, — then omits One Couplet — and then inserts another; and all these mutilated Limbs, thus preposterously jumbled together, and constituting one hideous Mass of Deformity, are very gravely contrasted with some lovely Lines from Pope's highly-finished Eloisa to Abelard. She then makes some more Extracts from Helen to Paris — selecting Two Lines — then jumping over Sixteen — then chusing Six more — linking them all together — and finally comparing them with some *other* beautiful Lines from Eloisa.

Miss Seward remarks ([*GM*] p. 524), that my "other Pleas, which seek to prove the Certainty that Dryden was *not* the Translator of the Epistle from Helen to Paris, *though he avows it* Solely *his through* All the Editions, are set aside by those Passages of *equal* Inelegance, which have been already cited in the Course of this Controversy, from the Hind and Panther, Ode on the Death of Anne Killigrew, the Virgil, and other of his Works."[213]

The Assertion, that Dryden avows the Epistle from Helen to Paris Solely his through All the Editions, is inaccurate. I had *before* asserted that the Names of the Poet and the Peer were United in that Production; and I had quoted a satyrical Couplet written on the Occasion:[214] Circumstances which, one should suppose, might have induced My Friend to have expressed a contrary Opinion with some *Hesitation* — Were I to take the Trouble of a Search, I should, probably, find twenty Editions that would confirm my Assertion; but *two* will suffice. In one, printed for Jacob Tonson in 1716 (the Property of Hugford Hassall, Esq.

of Solihull), and in another, printed for J. Tonson 1725 (belonging to the Rev. Mr. Blyth of the same Place), the Earl of Mulgrave's Name is joined to that of Dryden;[215] nor, to the best of my Recollection, did I ever see or hear of *any* Edition — the one which Miss Seward mentions excepted — in which they were disunited.

Whoever, Mr. Urban, will refer to your Magazine for January, p. 29,[216] will find that — far from "seeking to prove the Certainty that Dryden was *not* the Translator of the Epistle from Helen to Paris"[217] — I *only* sought to prove that he was not the Author of those Parts of that Epistle which Miss Seward has ascribed to him. I do not consider my supposed Plea as set aside by the Passages she quoted from the Hind and Panther, &c. — because I do *not* consider those Passages as "of equal Inelegance!"

Miss Seward's Notion, that, because I made "no Comment," I was "willing your Readers should *forget* them," is not founded. The Recollection of them could *not* have been "utterly destructive of my unfortunate Assertion, that the Style of the great Dryden is Never injudiciously debased"[218] — *because* I had made no such Assertion. My Words, in your Magazine for January, p. 27, were — "whatever may be found reprehensible in his Sentiments or Imagery — his Style, I will still Contend, is pure."[219] In the Preface to the Woodmen of Arden (p. 9), I said "Many of his Lines *seem*, 'tis true, to have wanted his last Touches; but those last Touches, I Am Persuaded, were not *hastily* Neglected — but *deliberately* Denied."[220]

Contending for the Propriety of a Persuasion is not equivalent to the *asserting* of a Fact; nor, if I *had* made such an Assertion, would the Quotations in Question have utterly destroyed it: — because ludicrous Imagery, incongruous Metaphor, and inconsistent Fable, are the Faults most conspicuous in those Passages; Matters with which I had Nothing to do; — "my Business being merely with his Diction."[221]

Joseph Weston.

(To be continued on our next.)

22.

Mr. Urban, *Nov.* 4. [1790]

[After some compliments to the combatants, Philip Thicknesse continues:] But it grieves me to see a man of rare talents, whose language is so correct, whose manners are so polished, and whose talents are so great, employed in endeavours to make Miss Seward publicly acknowledge what she and all the world know to be true; namely, that Pope was a paltry fellow. But Mr. W. may rest satisfied that she will never acknowledge it.

* * * *

Yours, &c. P. T.

23.

Mr. Urban,   *Edinburgh, Nov.* 9. [1790]

I am one among many of your numerous readers who cannot suppress my indignation at the cruel treatment the character of *Pope* continues to experience from one of your most respectable correspondents. I have beheld with pain the eager, but fruitless, efforts of that elegant writer to substantiate some charge that might criminate him.

But I believe a majority of your readers will agree with me, that what has been yet said or done are [sic] not sufficient to effect that purpose, and that the Poet has now, as heretofore, the multitude on his side. He is charged, but surely not with justice, with envy and hatred to *Dryden*; the man, of all others, whom he appears to have regarded with cordial esteem and affection, and to whom, in all his writings, he pays the most unequivocal homage. But it seems he suffered the gentle and compliant *Swift* to sneer at that great Poet's translation of Virgil, in a satyrical romance considered anonymous, I suppose, even by *Pope* himself. He is also accused of having satirized certain authors, rather too severely, in a poem called the *Dunciad*; but certainly not from envy, or fear of rivality; for who envies or fears those who are infinitely beneath them? We can crush a wasp with a touch, though it may hurt us with its sting.

* * * *

The *pharisaical Addison*, with a heart as cool as his writings, could be *really* guilty of the crime which *Pope* is accused of; and the *pious Johnson* well knew the use of the literary stiletto; yet *these* were certainly virtuous men. . . .

* * * *

It has of late become fashionable to lower the estimation which the writings of *Pope* were heretofore universally held in. This, however, will not change their qualities; for *de gustibus non est disputandum* is as applicable to poetical as to any other taste; and the poetry of *Pope* still continues to please *nine* out of *ten* readers, who can find no meaning in the *clinquant* of modern rhimers [sic].

118

If writers, whose fame is already established, are to be opposed to each other, they should be compared, like Plutarch's heroes, not with an intention of depreciating their merits, but of displaying their excellencies in the fullest point of view.   Yours, &c. W.

---

24. (continues Letter 21)
Continuation of Mr. Weston's Defence of the Preface to the Woodmen of Arden.

Solihull, Dec. 23. [1790]
Who, Mr. Urban, that reads Miss Seward's Remark, [*GM*] page 120, —viz. "to assert Dryden's Style *advantaged* by its frequent Vapidness and Vulgarity, is *but* to want Taste for pure and elegant Composition"²²² —would not take for granted that I had *really* made such an assertion? —And yet none such is to be found. —To assert that *any* Style could derive an Advantage from Vapidness would be indeed Want of Taste; but that a *certain Degree* of Vulgarity, *occasionally* introduced, is a Disadvantage, I am not quite so sure.

I will concede to my too fastidious Antagonist —that many Low expressions may be picked out of Dryden's Works; and let her make the most of this concession: it no way contradicts my Opinion of the *Purity* of Dryden's Style —An apt Example will save a World of Argument; and my Meaning will be sufficiently explained by a single couplet.

In the Opening of the celebrated Absalom and Achitophel we meet with the following lines.

> "When Man on Many multiplied his Kind,
> Ere One to One was, Cursedly, confin'd." [1:3-4]

Cursedly is *now*, and, probably, was *then*, a Low word. — "I am cursedly mortified" — "I was cursedly taken in" — are Modes of Speech in very frequent use among the vulgar; but were Miss Seward, on that score, to expel the honest, unaffected, and forcible expression, and to supply its place by one of her own elegant — or one of her Parnassian Brethren's *finical* Phrases — the Line would, in *my* Opinion, be *cursedly* injured. — "Fatally" — "cruelly" —and twenty other Substitutes *might* be found —and serve to *liquify* the Line, and lull tasteless Readers to Sleep; but Memory, trust me, might be ransacked long enough, before a Word would present itself so *nervously* descriptive of the Poet's Meaning as that Vulgar one which he has so judiciously chosen!

But to proceed. —Miss Seward quotes eight lines from Dryden's Charming Version of Dido to Eneas as challenging the "worst Lines in the Helen to Paris;" — "Lord Mulgrave," she says, "could not jingle couplets that less deserved the Name of Poetry;"[223] — let us examine the Justice of this Assertion.

But I shall take the Liberty of restoring to their Place four Lines, which Miss Seward has omitted, and of adding four more which complete the sense, and if Dryden's Translation shall not be found equal, at *least*, to his Original, I will for ever renounce all Pretensions to Knowledge or to Judgment.

First for Ovid.

Facta fugis; facienda petis, quaerenda per orbem
  Altera, quaesita est altera terra tibi.
Ut terram invenias, quis eam tibi tradet habendam?
  Quis sua non notis arva tenenda dabit?
Alter habendus amor tibi restat, & altera Dido:
  Quamque iterum fallas, altera danda fides.
Quando erit, ut condas instar Carthaginis urbem,
  Et videas populos altus ab arce tuos?
Omnia ut eveniant, nec te tua vota morentur;
  Unde tibi, quae te sic amet, uxor erit?
Uror, ut inducto ceratae sulfure taedae:
  Ut pia fumosis addita thura focis.
Aeneas oculis semper vigilantis inhaeret:
  Aenean animo noxque diesque refert.[224]

Dryden.

Built Walls you Shun, *unbuilt* you Seek; *that* Land
Is yet to Conquer; but you *this* Command.
Suppose you landed where your wish design'd,
Think what Reception *Foreigners* would find.
What People is so void of common Sense,
To vote Succession from a *Native* Prince?
Yet *there* new Scepters and new Loves you seek;
New Vows to plight, and plighted Vows to break.
When will your Tow'rs the height of *Carthage* know?
Or when your Eyes discern such Crowds below?
If such a *Town*, and *Subjects* you could see,
Still would you want a Wife — *who lov'd like me.*
For, oh, I burn, like Fires with Incense bright;
Not holy Tapers flame with purer Light:
Aeneas is my Thoughts perpetual Theme:
Their daily longing, and their nightly Dream. [1:13-28.]

Mulgrave*

On *Carthage* and its rising Walls you frown,
And shun a scepter, which is now your own;
All you have gain'd, you proudly do contemn,
And fondly seek a fancy'd Diadem.
And should you reach at last this promis'd Land,
Who'll give its Power into a Stranger's Hand?
Another easy *Dido* do you seek;
And new occasions new-made Vows to break?
When can you Walls like ours of *Carthage* build,
And see your Streets with Crowds of Subjects fill'd?
But tho' all this succeeded to your Mind,
So true a Wife no Search could ever find.
Scorch'd up with Love's fierce Fire my Life does waste,
Like Incense on the flaming Altar cast;
All Day *Aeneas* walks before my Sight;
In all my Dreams I see him ev'ry Night:[225]

To offer a single Observation on the respective Merits of the two
Translations would be to offer an Insult to every *Judge* of Poetry; — the
only Readers for whom I wish to write.

... to [Miss Seward's] Censure of Dryden's Translation of the same
Book I shall oppose the Opinion of Pope himself; who says, (in his
preface to the Iliad,) "had he translated the Whole Work† I would no
more have attempted Homer after him than Virgil, his Version of whom
(notwithstanding some human Errors) is the most noble and spirited
Translation I know in any Language." [7:22.]

* * * *

Meanwhile, I would not advise Miss Seward to be *too* hasty in her
Selection of Passages from Pope, to match with "the noblest and most
beautiful ones"[226] from his Master; lest a Misfortune should befal [sic]
her similar to one which happened to Spence: and it should be found,
that what she produces, as specimens of the Richness of that Genius
which she pronounces equal to Dryden's, should only add to the Proofs
already extant of his *Knack* at pilfering!

(*To be concluded in our next.*)

---

* My Reasons for conjecturing that He was the Author of the second
Version of Dido to Aeneas were given in the Magazine for January, p.
30. [Letter 8d.]

† He translated only the first Book, and a small part of the Sixth. [Hector's last parting from Andromache, 1:846.]

25.

Mr. Urban, Nov. 30. [1790]

Every one, at all acquainted with modern poetry and criticism, well knows that one of the principal embellishments of the comic epopee is the introduction of parodies on passages in ancient and modern classicks. If Pope, among the host of bad or party-writers who attacked his fame, had not been able to discover a *pair* who wrote against him in *partnership*, he would have lost the opportunity of introducing a parody on the young Chiefs who form the subject of the most interesting episode, if episode it ought to be called, in the Aeneid. But, luckily for our Poet, one Burnet and Ducket published a joint-work against his first undertaking to translate the Iliad, intituled, "Homerides, by Sir Iliad Doggrel;"[227] and furnished him with a Nisus and a Euryalus for his Dunciad. It is in the games in honour of Anchises that the young heroes first make their appearance.

> Nisus & Euryalus primi.
> Euryalus *forma insignis viridique juventa*;
> Nisus *amore pio pueri.*   Aen.V. 296.[228]

And when they appear in the character of warriors, we are told,

> Nisus erat *portae custos,*
> Et juxta comes Euryalus. —
> His *amor unus* erat, *pariterque in bella ruebant,*
> Tunc quoque *communi portam statione tenebant.*   Aen.IX.183.[229]

Let us now see how Pope profited by these passages. Elkanah Settle, after regretting to Cibber how unfortunate it was that two such great men of their party as Dennis and Gildon[230] should wage war with each other, addresses himself to the shades of those great Criticks, in a parody on the beautiful lines in the Aeneid alluding to Caesar and Pompey:

> Embrace, embrace, my sons! be foes no more!
> Nor glad vile Poets with true Criticks' gore*.
>
> [*DunA* 5:3.171-72.]

By way of contrast, he points out to Cibber the friendship of two others:

> Behold yon pair, in *strict embraces* join'd†;
> How *like* in manners, and how *like* in *mind*!

Fam'd for good-nature Burnet, *and for truth;*
Ducket *for pious passion to the youth*††
Equal in wit, and equally polite,
Shall this a Pasquin, that a Grumbler write.
Like are their merits, like rewards they share;
That shines a *consul,* that commissioner.   [*Dun*A 5:3.173-80.]

The Critick Dennis, a fellow sufferer, as we have seen, in the cause, with the ingenuity of a commentator accustomed to find meanings his author never thought of, insinuated in print,[231] that Pope had, in the above parody, attacked the moral characters of Burnet and Ducket. But it is plain that the persons themselves were not such *Dunces* as to misunderstand the Poet. If the charge had been true, the crime, rendered notorious by the celebrity of accuser, must have obliged them to leave their country; and, if false, a jury would undoubtedly have adjudged heavy damages for so atrocious a calumny. But they were too wise either to fly their country, or appeal to a jury; for, had they had recourse to the latter, I think we may safely pronounce what would have been the event in the words of Pope and Horace:

Solventur risu tabulae, tu missus abibis.[232]
In such a case the plaintiff will be hiss'd,
My Lords the Judges laugh, and you're dismiss'd.

[*HS* 4:2.i.155-56.]

Such is my view of the above passage, on which a late writer in your Magazine, who stands forward as the professed accuser of Pope and defender of the heroes of the Dunciad, has founded his grand charge against him. This writer, in your present volume, p. 388, asserts, that, "in consequence of the Colonel's (Ducket's) spirited conduct on this extraordinary attack, Pope found it *convenient* to add the following note."[233] M. F. (Ib. p. 786) asks, *What was the Colonel's spirited conduct on this occasion?*[234] Mr. W. has replied to the letter of M. F. but has omitted to answer the above question. This I now call upon him to do.

* * * *

Yours, &c. J. S.

---

*   Ne pueri ne tanta animis assuescite [adsuescite] bella:
Neu patriae validas in viscera vertite vires. Aen. VI. 833. ["O my sons, make not a home within your hearts for such warfare, not upon your country's very vitals turn her vigour and valour," 6.832-33.]

123

† Illae autem paribus quas fulgere cernis in armis *Concordes animae.* Ib. 826. ["But they whom thou seest gleaming in equal arms, souls harmonious now," 6.826-27.]

†† *Amore pio* pueri.

---

26. (continues Letter 24)
Continuation of Mr. Weston's Defence of the Preface to the Woodmen of Arden.

Dec. 23, 1790.

In that Essay on the Odyssey which, affected and superficial as it is, gained Spence much Reputation among the Admirers of Pope, he observes:

> "In these last Volumes, how finely are some Thoughts wove into this Translation from the sacred Pages? from the Iliad, and Aeneid; from Dryden, and Milton among ourselves; and from several others, both Ancient and Moderns?
>
> "The Translator is sometimes as Artful in adding, of himself, some short Strokes to what Homer has said. We meet with several of these little insertions, which are very just and improving. I shall mention but one. As Mr. Addison proposes a Correction of Paradise Lost, by cutting off the two last Lines; Mr. Pope improves this Poem, by adding a Line in the Conclusion of it: This Insertion possibly is better chose, than that Alteration so modestly proposed by Mr. Addison. The Reader, indeed, would willingly go off with some Hopes and Satisfaction, after the melancholy Scene in Milton's last Book: but it may be said that, considering the moral and chief Design of that Poem, Terror is the last Passion to be left upon the Mind of the Reader. On the contrary, the Odyssey ought on all Accounts to terminate happily: and Mr. Pope's Addition, in the Close of it, is therefore an Improvement, because it forwards the Moral; it gives us a fuller* View and Confirmation of the Happiness of Ulysses, and leaves it upon a firmer Foundation."[235]

'Tis not easy for any one, who recollects the last Line of Absalom and Achitophel,[236] to restrain a Smile, at this pompous Parade — The Critic, by professing to give this Line as one of those "short Strokes" which Pope added of Himself, proclaims his Unconsciousness of his being indebted to Dryden for *every Syllable* of this boasted Improvement on Homer![237]

[Weston reiterates his opposition to Miss Seward's main points about Pope's superiority to Dryden: his "harmonious and flowing Verses" (Letter 10) and his closed couplets.]

... and so, because Pope's Verses *exhibit* no great Variety in the Flow of the Numbers, every succeeding Writer in the couplet Measure is condemned, like a Squirrel in a Cage, to jingle his ten Bells in the same everlasting Tune!

"Mr. Morfitt calls Pope's Numbers 'Cuckoo-notes.'"[238] — True. — He does so. — So does Welsted.[239] — So do I. (I am not ashamed of the Association) — And what then? — Miss Seward "is incapable of being cloyed with them. — Very likely. — She has an indisputable Right to dine *entirely* on Sweetmeats, if she pleases; but must they who deem Beef and Pudding comfortable Additions be stigmatized for Prejudice and Want of Taste?

To conclude all which I think necessary to say in Vindication of that Part of my Preface to the Woodmen of Arden which asserts the Superiority of Dryden's Versification over that of Pope and of the Moderns.

Miss Seward seems to think that a Poet, like an Asiatic Monarch, should never descend from his Dignity; — never be visible, unless surrounded with the Paraphernalia of Royalty: while I — (so essentially different is our Taste!) have felt as much sincere Respect, as much loyal Affection, for our gracious Monarch, when I have seen him, in Boots and Leather Breeches, conversing with his Attendants, with that endearing Condescention, and fascinating Affability, so conspicuous in his Character, as ever I felt when I have beheld him, seated on his Throne, in all the Pageantry of State, and looking (as old Lear expresses it) "every Inch a King!"[240]

Miss Seward is therefore perfectly right, in withdrawing from a Contest, in which neither of us is likely to become a Convert to the other's Opinion.

The Remainder of these Observations will be devoted to the Vindication of that Part of my Preface which respects Pope's Moral Character.

[Weston again insists that Pope's baseness of character alone made him a "Tormentor of minds and Murderer of Reputations." He vehemently rejects the arguments to the contrary that the other correspondents have made. Weston maintains that Pope's tyranny continues to blight poetry.]

Perfectly convinced *myself*, I trust that I shall ultimately convince Thousands of your *Readers*; if I should be disappointed in that Expectation, I shall wrap myself in the Consciousness of my benevolent Intentions: and, being no Cormorant of Praise, I shall think myself amply rewarded for my Labour by the Approbation of the Candid and the Discerning; and, with Respect to the Rest, I shall only say, "Si Populus Vult decipi — Decipiatur**."   Yours, &c. Joseph Weston.

_____

*"So Pallas spoke: The mandate from above
The King obey'd. The Virgin-seed of Jove
In Mentor's form confirm'd the full accord,
And willing nations knew their lawful Lord.
[*Od* 10:24.628-31. The final line is enclosed in quotation marks.]

"Homer himself does not end in so full and complete a manner: his last line does not rest well; and Chapman seems resolved to shew the infirmness of it as much as he could possibly in his Translation, which breaks off in these lines:

" — — twixt both parts the seed of Jove,
Athenian Pallas, of all future love
A league compos'd; and for her form took choice
Of Mentor's likeness, both in limb and voice."

[George Chapman, *The Twenty-Fourth Book of Homer's Odysseys*, last 4 lines]

** "If [Since] the World will — why — Let it be deceiv'd." *Conscious Lovers.* [Sir Richard Steele, III.434.]

27.
Mr. Urban,   *Solihull, Jan.* 3, 1791.
[Weston begins by attacking "J.S.'s" letter (No. 25), charging that he "wastes nearly two Columns — only to prove, at last, my Charge against Pope Well-Founded."] He — who has so slender an Acquaintance with the Subject on which he writes, as to be yet to learn that Ducket Did understand "pious Passion" to convey a scandalous Aspersion, and, by Threats of "Personal Chastisement," obliged Pope to substitute "cordial Friendship" in its Room, and to add a solemn Disavowal of his malignant Meaning: He — who, by terming a Remark — "an Appeal," changes Decency into Indelicacy, and Creates an Inconsistency where he cannot Find one — may take my Word for it, that "he never *shall* force himself upon me for an Adversary."[241]   J. W.

28.
Mr. Urban,   *Oct.* 27. [1790]
I have been for some time sickened with the affected and verbose invectives against Pope of Mr. Weston, whose incorrigible absurdity,

and inveterate malignity against that great poet, are so conspicuous, as almost to justify the expressions I have made use of.

Disquisitions of this kind are in their nature capable of mathematical demonstration; and as Mr. W's perversion of intellect seems to incapacitate him for conviction of any sort, but such as appeals to the senses, my indignation would have evaporated in silence, had he not in your last Magazine, p. 780,[242] advanced a position which may be refuted by chronology([1]), and of the falsehood of which, therefore, even he must be convinced.

Pope, says Mr. W, incited([2]) Swift to ridicule Dryden in "The Tale of a Tub,"([3]) and "Battle of the Books."

One must be very little acquainted with Swift's character, to suppose for a moment that he would permit Pope to direct his pen upon any subject. One must be very ignorant not to know, that Swift's aversion to Dryden arose from a personal disgust([4]); and that Pope, as Dr. Johnson himself relates, always vindicated Dryden from the censures of Addison, *and praised him through his whole life with unvaried liberality*([5]).

But these observations are intended for readers of another turn of mind than Mr. W.; who may however, it is possible, be ashamed([6]) when he reads that Swift was born in 1667, Pope not till 1688. Before 1688 Swift's chamberfellow is said to have seen a copy of "The Tale of a Tub" in his own handwriting([7]). Dr. Johnson thinks it was written between 1693 and 1697; and (not to trouble ourselves with considering when, or by whom, it was *written*), we all know that it was *published* in 1704. The consequences in favour of Pope's innocence arising from this chronological deduction are obvious. Pope was born in the year when Swift's chum saw a copy of the work which Mr. W. supposes him to have dictated; he was from five to nine years of age when Dr. Johnson([8]) thinks it was written; and when it was printed he was sixteen. At what period the acquaintance of these great men commenced, I have not learned; but it certainly was not till after this time, because Pope had not then published his Pastorals, with which his literary life commenced([9]); and we know that he was recommended to the notice of Swift by his growing celebrity only, which could not have been till some time after 1704.

After this, I shall leave Pope's vindication from Mr. W's other equally unmerited charges to abler hands.

> Accipe..... insinias [insidias], & crimine ab uno
> Disce omnes.[243]

Yours, &c. B. L. A.

(¹) Dr. Bentley (Dissert. on Phalaris, p. 122, [Richard Bentley, *Dissertations upon the Epistles of Phalaris*, ed. Wilhelm Wagner (London, 1883) 121-22.]) justly considers the argument, drawn from discrepancy of time, to be the most conclusive which can be adduced on subjects of this nature: and in conformity hereunto Cicero says, "Non tu quidem *tota* re [I cannot say so much for Mr. Weston], sed *quod maximum est*, Temporibus errasti." Philipp. 2da. ["here you are mistaken, not indeed in the facts as a whole, but — what is most important — in the dates," *Philippics* 2, p.87.] παρ οις ασυναρτητος εστιν η των χρονων αναγραφη, says Titian, παρα τουτοις ουδε τα της ιστοριας αληθευειν δυναται. ["Among people whose record of time is disjointed," says Tatian, "not even the facts of history can be true" (Eusebius, *Scripta Ecclesiastica et Theologica: Praeparatio Evangelica*, 10.11.5.4-6)] The name "Titian" in the original footnote is a misprint. For discovering this as well as providing the source and the translation, I am indebted to Peter Smith and George Marsden.

Judicis officium est, ut res, ita Tempora rerum Quaerere. ["It is the duty of one who exercises judgment to inquire both into the facts and their chronology." Unidentified.]

(²) This is a rather stronger expression than that used by Mr. Weston. Edit. [Weston wrote, "To prove that Pope really *did* suffer his Friends to depreciate the Person from whom he learned *all that is valuable*... Miss Seward cannot forget Swift," Letter 18.]

(³) I have long had doubts of Swift's title to this work; and my suspicions are much confirmed by observing that Dr. Johnson (as Mr. Boswell, in his Journal, tells us,) entertained the same idea. [Johnson stated, "I doubt whether the "Tale of a Tub" be his (Swift's); for he never owned it, and it is much above his usual manner." *Boswell's Life of Johnson*, ed. G. B. Hill (Oxford: Clarendon, 1934). 1:452. Boswell recorded Johnson's repetition of this opinion at 2:318-319 and at greater length at 5:44.] This was, however, an *esoterick* doctrine of the Doctor; for, in his "Lives of the Poets," he does not hint at such a thing. [In the *Life of Swift*, Johnson temporized judicially: "That Swift was its (*Tale of a Tub*'s) author, though it be universally believed, was never owned by himself, nor ever well proved by any evidence; but no other claimant can be produced, and he did not deny it when Archbishop Sharpe and the Duchess of by shewing it to the Queen, debarred him from a bishoprick." *Lives* 3:10.] It is certain that Swift never owned the work; which, to those who consider how much Swift prized his reputation as a man of wit, and how little he regarded the opinion which the world entertained of his religious character, will appear pretty extraordinary: and I think there is more learning in this than Swift has displayed in any of his avowed publications, together with a very different strain of humour. I have been inclined to give the work to Mr. Anthony Henley (father of Lord Chancellor Northington); a man of wit and learning, as appears by the IXth and Xth letters of "Swift's Correspondence," [*The Correspondence of Jonathan Swift, D.D.*, ed. F. Elrington Ball (London: G. Bell and Sons, 1910) 1:112-15] and to whom Dr. Garth dedicated "the Dispensary." He was, however, the patron of Dennis, and assisted him in his plays. [Henley (d. 1711) was a wit and friend of Swift's. There is no evidence that he wrote *Tale of a Tub*. His son Robert was Lord Chancellor to George III, who made him Earl of Northington in 1764.]

(⁴) When Swift shewed to Dryden some specimens of his early poetry, which are, to be sure, very bad, "Cousin Swift," said Dryden, as he returned him his papers, "you will never make a poet." [*Lives* 3 (Swift):7] Hence Swift's sarcasms.

(⁵) Lives, vol. IV. p 168. [*Lives*, 3:220.]

(⁶) Crebillon, it is true, says, that some men are as incapable of being ashamed of thinking wrong, as they are incapable of thinking right. Agaremens de Coeur, par.2da. [Claude Prosper Jolyot de Crebillon, *Les Egaremens du Coeur et de L'Esprit*, trans. by Barbara Bray as *The Wayward Head and Heart* (London: Oxford UP, 1963) possibly p. 154. Because of the difference in translations, I have been unable to find "B. L. A.'s" exact words.]

(⁷) Dean Swift, p. 21. [Irvin Ehrenpreis cites evidence that the *Tale* "was mainly composed about 1696," *Swift: The Man, His Works, and the Age* (London: Methuen, 1967) 2:333. Ehrenpreis also mentions the belief of Swift's eighteenth-century biographer, John Lyon, that several people saw a draft of the *Tale* in Swift's handwriting while he was at Trinity College, Dublin (1682-1686) 1:186n.]

(⁸) Lives of the English Poets, vol. III. p. 388. [Johnson places *The Tale of a Tub*'s composition "in the four years that passed between his (Swift's) return (to Sir William Temple's employ) and Temple's death"; *ie.*, 1696-99 not 1693-97 as "B.L.A." says. *Lives*, 3:7 and note 5. Johnson gives its publication date as 1704 (3:10).]

(⁹) Ib. vol. IV. p. 12. [*Lives* 3:94.]

29.

Mr. Urban,   *Flintshire, Sept.* 22. [1790]

* * * *

... but I could not resist the opportunity of publishing my sentiments respecting two Poets deservedly held very high in the estimation of their country. However loth I may be to differ from a lady of Miss Seward's acknowledged taste, and although I admire Pope very much, I must candidly confess that, upon the whole, I subscribe to Mr. Weston's opinion; and think Dryden most certainly merited a more exalted seat in the Temple of Fame than his rival. One of your correspondents has observed, that he could never read two hundred *pages* of Pope without satiety.[244] For my part, two hundred *lines* at one time, however admirable in point of rhyme and cadence, are enough to disgust my ears with their unvaried melody and uniformity of construction: no flats, nor sharps; no happy mixture of discord; no spirit or fermentation of thought or numbers, produced by a due combination of sweets and acids; few Alexandrines, or triplets (which I think very essential, at least in a poem of any length), to break the constant monotony of the *cuckow* — no, the *blackbird*-notes, so warmly vindicated by Miss Seward.[245] Dryden, on the other hand, it must be confessed, even by Mr. Weston, is frequently too careless, and very unequal in his versification: "Nil fuit unquam sic impar *sibi.*"[246] But in regard to genius, originality, conception, strength, and sublimity, there surely can be no comparison! Pope, if I may be allowed the expression, may be said to offend by his *perfection*; Dryden, to please by his *imperfection*. I say nothing of Pope's moral character, because, in my opinion, *that* has nothing to do with the subject in dispute; which I conceive at its commencement to have been, not which of the two was the better *Man*, but the better *Poet*.

* * * *

Yours, &c. R. W.

Or, Bardus Ordovicensis. [Poet of North Wales][247]

30.

Mr. Urban,   *Nov.* 27. [1790]

Mr. Pope's character may safely be trusted in the hands of so able an advocate as Miss Seward; and her defence will be no difficult business, if what those who best knew him have affirmed, be true; "His meanest talent was his wit."[248]

As to Welsted, his patience under an infamous calumny was wonderful in a man so irritable as he is represented, and so admirably qualified to revenge the affront.

Full ten yerrs [years] slander'd, did he once reply?
Three thousand suns went down on Welsted's lie.

[*EpArb* 4:374-75.]

Yours, &c. R. B.

31.

Nevhailes, near
Mr. Urban,   *Edinburgh, Jan.*1. [1791]
   Had the controversy, as to Dryden and Pope, been carried on by
inferior writers, the publick might have been entertained with it as long
as the antagonists had any literary ammunition left of paper and ink.
But it must give pain to considerate readers, when they see persons of
genius bestowing *that* time in fruitless altercation, which they might
employ more worthily, and more usefully. Will the combatants agree to
an *armistice* for twelve months, on the principle of *uti possidetis*?[249] I dare
say that, after the lapse of that term, neither party will be disposed to
renew hostilities.
   The cause of Pope's censure is said to have originated from a
pamphlet, entitled "Homerides."[250] I will not assert positively, but I
think that the pamphlet was not aimed against Mr. Pope, or his
translation of Homer, which, by the way, is no more to Homer, than I to
Hercules. It is, if I mistake not, a catalogue of the last House of Commons
in the reign of Queen Anne, composed in burlesque rhymes. As the
author was a zealous Whig, it may well be supposed that he did not spare
the Tory friends of Mr. Pope.[251]

* * * *

Dav. Dalrymple. [Lord Hailes]

32.

Mr. Urban,   *Solihull, Feb.*22. [1791]
   [Weston indignantly defends himself against "B.L.A.'s" charge that
he is "*affected* and *verbose*" and prone to "incorrigible *Absurdity* and
inveterate malignity" (Letter 28). All quotations from "B.L.A." are from
this letter. Weston has added the emphasis and capitals.]
   But what Is this Position, — so demonstrative of my inveterate Malignity? "Pope (says Mr. W.) Incited Swift to ridicule Dryden in 'The Tale
of a Tub,' and 'Battle of the Books.'"

131

In Verity, Mr. Urban, if I Had advanced any such Position, I must have been — not only the maddest of all Madmen — but, also, the most foolish of all Fools; for well do I remember that the express Purpose of the entire Page to which B.L.A. adverts was to vindicate myself from a *similar* Charge brought against me by Miss Seward — viz. that I had accused Pope of "having meanly Influenced his Friends to exalt his Compositions above their just Level, for the Purpose of lowering Dryden's and tearing the Laurels from his Brow."[252]

Do me the Favour, Mr. Urban, to remark the pointed Manner in which I disclaimed the imputed Intention.

> * "I meant only to affirm, that Pope's *Friends* practiced insidious Arts, with a View to undermine the Reputation of the deceased Poet, and to asperse the Characters of his living Supporters; and that He *suffered* them so to do; — I did Not say *instigated* — I did Not say *assisted*; merely Suffered: — and I thought that I had expressed my Meaning so clearly as not to *admit* of Misconstruction; but I was mistaken."

After so strenuously declaring that I never meant to affirm that Pope Instigated — to have affirmed, *in the same Page*, that he Incited any of his Friends to ridicule Dryden, would have been droll enough! — Language so *very* explicit one would imagine left no Room for Misapprehension; but *humanum est errare* — A Reference to the Paragraph (p. 780).[253] which B.L.A. so candidly and so *correctly* quotes will prove that — to *whatever* Quarter "Malignity" and "Falsehood" may be ascribed — they cannot with any great Propriety be attributed to Me.

> "To prove that Pope really *did* suffer his Friends to depreciate the Person from whom he learned *all that is valuable* in the *Structure* of his Verse were a very easy task indeed. — To mention only One (but that one an Host!). — Miss Seward cannot forget Swift — the Partner of Pope's Labours and the Friend of his Bosom; — nor can she forget his Comparison of Dryden's Virgil to a Mouse under a Canopy of State: no — nor his grave assertion in his Dedication of his Tale of a Tub to Prince Posterity:
> "[']I do affirm, upon the Word of a sincere Man, that there is now actually in Being a certain Poet, called John Dryden, whose Translation of Virgil was lately printed in large Folio, well-bound, and, if diligent Search were made, for aught I know, is yet to be seen.'"

Here, Mr. Urban, you find my Complaint against Pope to be — *not* that he incited — but — that he Suffered Swift to ridicule that Work which Pope himself pronounced to be "the most noble and spirited Translation he knew in any Language."[254]

B.L.A. *asserts* ([*GM*] p. 1178) that I suppose Pope to have Dictated the Tale of a Tub; but so far was I from entertaining any such absurd Supposition that, in your Magazine for November (p.974.) I continued my Observations on Pope's Conduct, in the following Manner.

"But how (Miss Seward may ask) can Pope be to blame? — Could He prevent Swift's Attack on Dryden any more than She could prevent mine on Pope? — Probably Not; but He might have acted on that Occasion as She has on one nearly similar — viz. have called *his* Friend to a public Account for his 'Prejudice' and 'Want of Taste.' — My generous Assailant must surely allow that either she has done *too much* or he — *too little!*"[255]

These Quotations, I fancy, will be *more* than sufficient to exculpate me from the Imputations of inveterate Malignity, and wilful Falsehood; and, if I Do feel Shame, on this Occasion (of which B.L.A. obligingly allows the Bare Possibility), I certainly do *not* feel it on my Own Account!

By the Way, Mr. Urban, might it not tend to *prevent*, or, at least, to *shorten* Disputes, if Critics, before they presumed to *write*, would condescend to *read*? In the present Case, however, the Neglect of that Precaution has been eventually fortunate for your Readers; for — had B.L.A. *but* Read — he, probably, would not have Written: and then — what a delicious Olio of classical, critical, and chronological Knowledge would the Literary World have lost!
                                                            Joseph Weston.

___
* See Vol. LX. p. 780. [Letter 18.]

___

33.

Mr. Urban,   *Yarmouth, March 5.* [1791]

Your Correspondent Mr. Weston, after he has been disarmed, and thrown to earth, struggling in vain to wound the genius and character of the illustrious Pope, like Garrick's Richard[256] stabbing the air at the feet of Richmond, affords melancholy proof of the strength of Prejudice, debasing a mind which Imagination has adorned, and on which Benevolence is allowed to have often shed her kindest influence.

Mr. W. is furiously angry at a letter in your last Supplement, which does most certainly ruin his cause by disarming the force of all the evidence which he can produce to destroy the general esteem in which the memory of that exquisite Poet, that warm, Friend, that tender and pious Son, is deservedly held: notwithstanding his too keen irritability when the envious Troop threw their feeble darts against a shield of proof.

B.L.A.'s letter is fatal to Mr. Weston, because whenever a person has given, or at least refuses to *retract* an accusation, of which the accused is proved innocent, every previous and succeeding evidence from such an inveterate enemy, naturally and inevitably lose all force upon Minds of free and candid enquiry.

Behold a passage from Mr. Weston's comment in your last Mag. upon B.L.A.'s *undoing* Letter.

"Here Mr. Urban you find my complaint against Pope to be, not that he Incited, but that he Suffered Swift to ridicule the Work, which Pope himself pronounced to be the most noble and spirited Translation that he knew in any language."[257]

B.L.A.'s letter observes that Dr. Johnson avows his belief that the Tale of a Tub, which contains that ridiculous spite of Swift's to the great Dryden, was written in an interval when Pope was between five and nine years old.[258] He proves that it was published when Pope was only sixteen — yet Mr. Weston takes no shame to himself for having imputed it as a proof of Pope's badness of heart that he did not influence Swift to suppress it — What! — Could a Child of nine years old, or a young Poet of sixteen, possess the power of influencing the proudest Man existing, concerning what he should, or should *not* write!!!

The word Suffer, applied to Swift, not only respecting such a Child as Pope then was, but in reference to any Human Being, is even more ridiculous than Incite. An Infant might *possibly* tell Swift something which might incite him to anger, or might soften his resentment; but it is impossible to suppose a Man of his matchless pride, and obstinacy dependant upon the Sufferance of any man living respecting his Writings.

Mr. Weston's logic that either Miss Seward had done too much in defending Pope against himself, or Pope too little in not defending Dryden against Swift is demonstrably fallacious from the evident difference of their respective situations. Swift was twenty-one years older than Pope — his reputation established — his wit awing [sic] the whole literary world — his moroseness and the proof his injustice to Dryden afforded of unsubsiding resentments: *these* considerations may be supposed to have operated *wisely* upon Pope to let the malevolent and impotent sneer, from the pen of Swift, remain through life unnoticed: his *own* noble-minded praise sufficiently evincing how much he disdained the malice of his friend: expressions of contempt for Dryden equally virulent and equally powerless, may be found in Lord Shaftesbury's Characteristicks[259] — not merely against particular passages and whole bombast plays, which lie open to the censure of *all* just Taste, but against the Author as a man of genius, and against the whole of his compositions where good and bad, sublime and fustian, are so strangely mingled: and where the excellencies are so *noble*, as to atone for all the defects, prodigious as they are.

I apprehend Miss S. had no such reason to be silent upon attacks more virulent on Pope, from the Pen of a Man she *respected*, but not *feared*. Perhaps Mr. Weston was not *her* senior as to age: she probably did not believe him such an unforgiving Despot, as Pope knew Swift to be. Mr. W. threw down the gauntlet against the genius and worth of a writer she adored. That she took it up does not convict herself of presumption, or Pope of baseness, because *he* suffered Swift's to lie unnoticed on the ground, being in so very different line of connexion with the Offender.

Mr. Weston's advice to B.L.A. to *read* before he writes must put every body in mind of a very vulgar proverb about a Pot and Kettle. If Mr. W. had read before he wrote, he had not thus exposed himself by vilifying Pope at nine years old for Suffering Swift to write that ridiculous sarcasm or at sixteen for Suffering him to print it.

B.L.A.'s letter is accurate in point of information: it makes no display of classical knowledge: it does not contain one word of criticism: but it speaks with the most convincing good sense concerning the inference inevitable alike upon that accusation against Pope, whether the word *incited* or *suffered* be applied: and this from the plain chronological facts it states. Mr. Weston, in sneer, calls that letter "an olio of *classical, critical,* and *chronological* knowledge," as if it had made false pretences to all three. To the two first it makes *no* pretences: and there must be proof that it quotes *false dates* before his satire can affect the last: your Readers must have remarked how fortunately for the fame of the accused and for the defensive arguments, Mr. Weston's indiscreet violence lays him open, on every hand, to the contempt of the Severe, and the pity of the Candid. Truth and Justice, calmly secure in their own native strength, never lose their dignity in vehement invective.

Some of your Correspondents seem as deficient in memory, as Mr. W. in chronological knowledge, when they wish to see the controversy ended between Miss S. and Mr. W. the former having declared, in your Mag. for June last,[260] her resolve to drop it.

Satisfied with having demonstrated that Dryden often wrote wretchedly, and that Pope was clear of every cause of suspicion that he wished to lessen the fame of his admired Predecessor, nothing her Antagonist has *since* said upon the subject, was likely to induce her to alter her resolution. The poison, like Swift's exercised upon Dryden, carries its own Antidote.

135

Mr. Weston may spare his comments upon Pope's abuse of Lady M. W. Montague.[261] Its coarseness and personality were unjustifiable, be the provocation what it might. *Every* body allows it;[262] and all Mr. W. can say upon *that* subject is but like writing to prove the darkness of a moonless Midnight: but Midnight has its Morning; and Pope had recompensing virtues, chasing and brightening the gloom of that error.

Yours, &c. Norfolciensis. [John Aikin?]

34.

Mr. Urban,   *March* 16. [1791]

Not for the sake of the *mighty dead*,[263] but in compassion to the humble living readers of your valuable Repository, have pity on the manes of Dryden and Pope. Mr. Weston may spare his temper, and his labours; Pope will be read long after he will be forgotten. — He says triumphantly, Miss Seward may dine upon sweets, but he likes substantial food. I should be glad to ask his cook, whether he orders her to make the sauce *bad*, that the dinner may be completely *good?* — The controversy may be very grateful to the disputants, but it is very tiresome to many of your readers.   Yours, &c. D. R.

35.

Mr. Urban,   *Solihull, April* 15. [1791]

The Cause which flies for Aid to Artifice and Misrepresentation can be in no very flourishing Condition. — Of the one I have already convicted your Correspondent B.L.A. ([*GM*] p.139);[264] and I shall presently convict his Vindicator Norfolciensis of an Artifice even more reprehensible than *direct* Misrepresentation: because — to present *Truth* to the Eye, and to convey it *Opposite* to the Understanding — is the more dangerous, in Proportion as it is the less liable to Detection.

[Weston restates his objections to anonymous correspondents such as "B.L.A." and "Norfolciencis." He repeats that he wrote Pope suffered, not incited, his friends to exalt his compositions and to lower Dryden's.]

But some may wonder why B.L.A. and his zealous Assistant should take such *disgraceful* Pains to convict me of bringing a Charge against their Favourite, which I *never brought* — of trival Importance compared with *that* which I actually *did* bring, and which neither of them have made the slightest Attempt to disprove! — A Motive is suggested, [*GM*] p.224:[265]

"B.L.A's. Letter is fatal to Mr. Weston, Because whenever a Person has given, or at least refuses to *retract* an Accusation, of which the Accused is proved innocent, *every* Previous and Succeeding *Evidence* from such an inverterate Enemy, naturally and inevitably *lose* All Force upon Minds of free and candid Enquiry."

So, if the Crime of refusing to retract One unjust Accusation could have been *fixed* upon me, by *any* Means, *every* Previous, *every* Succeeding *Evidence*, respecting *other* Accusations — however reasonable, however incontestable — was to stand for Nothing!

Most idle and delusory Expectation!
"Most lame and impotent Conclusion!"[266]

Had I treated Pope as his Avengers have treated Me, I readily grant that I could not have hoped for much *future* Confidence in my Word; but, as the Evidence which I have brought against him was his Own and of Course fixed and permanent, (for Scripta Manent) I do not see how my Want of Veracity (had it been proved) could have affected my Argument. — Some Danger might, indeed, have been apprehended from the Probability of False Quotation; but the insulted Public, justly alarmed, would have regarded *my* Extracts with as wary an Eye, as they will, henceforth, any Quotations which B.L.A. or Norfolciensis may be pleased to make!

[Weston accuses his opponents of forcing him to procrastinate his proofs of Pope's bad character.]

Meanwhile the Trial of Pope is suspended; my Chain of Evidence is broken; my Train of Reasoning interrupted. Then comes in some petty Auxiliary, with his palty Jest, and his pert Exclamation — that "the Controversy is become Tiresome!"[267] — Throwing, *systematically*, perpetual Rubs in my Way, my generous Adversaries affect to wonder at the Slowness of my Progress!

* * * *

With your Leave, therefore, Mr. Urban, my Letter relative to Pope and Lady Mary shall be yet once more postponed; and that Letter, next Month, shall close the Business — For The Present; — resume it I Shall: but in a Way more likely to forward my upright Design.[268]

After I have, (Without Interruption,) in a Pamphlet[269] of which I shall think it my Duty to apprize your Readers, fully stated Pope's Evidence Against Himself, (and to *state* will be to *convict*,) the whole hostile Phalanx may discharge their hoarded Shafts — and welcome*! — My Point will have been established — my Cause — gained; — and the Cavils

137

and the Clamours of a Myriad of ignorant, stupid, or malicious Critics will avail no more than Pebbles hurled against the Monument!

To examine yet further your *Yarmouth* Correspondent's Remarks.

"B.L.A's letter is accurate in point of information."[270]—Of this Accuracy my letter [*GM*] p. 139[271] pointed out *one* shining instance, and I shall presently produce *another*. —It makes no display of *classical* knowledge: it does not contain one word of ["]criticism:" —consult "Johnson's Dictionary" (if necessary) for the meaning of the words classical and critical,[272] then consult the text and notes of B.L.A's Epistle ! —"But it speaks with the most convincing good-sense concerning the inference inevitably alike upon that accusation against Pope, whether the word *incited* or *suffered* be applied: and this from the plain chronological facts it states." —To the "convincing good sense" I have *already* replied; and to the "plain chronological facts" I am *going* to reply: —but first for a little more of quotation.

["]Mr. Weston, in sneer, calls that letter 'an Olio of *classical, critical* and *chronlogical knowledge*,' as if it had made false pretences to all three. To the two first it makes *no* pretences: (Again!) and there must be proof that it quotes *false dates* before his satire can affect the last:" —Indeed? —May not, then, a "Chronological Deduction," — even supposing it does *not* "quote false dates," become ridiculous, from the pomposity of its introduction, and the grossness of its misapplication.

However, if proofs of "false dates" Must be produced, they Shall.

**"But these observations are intended for readers of another turn of mind than Mr. W. who may However, it is Possible, be ashamed when he reads that Swift was born in 1667, Pope Not Till 1688. Before 1688 Swift's Chamber-fellow is *said* to have seen a copy of "The Tale of a Tub" in his own hand-writing. Dr. Johnson *thinks* it was written between 1693 and 1697: and (not to trouble ourselves with considering when, or by whom, it was *written*), we all know that it was *published* in 1704. The consequences in favour of Pope's innocence arising from this Chronological Deduction are obvious. Pope was born In the year when Swift's Chum saw a copy of the work, which Mr. W. supposes him to have dictated; he was from five to nine years of age when Dr. Johnson *thinks* it was written: and when it was printed he was sixteen."

This "undoing" piece of chronology — so "ruinous" to my cause — so "fatal" to my fame — is certainly (to use the words of one of the characters in Foote's Bankrupt) "finely confused" but surely *not* "very alarming!"[273] —At the *Commencement*, we are informed that Pope was *not* born Till 1688; and that Swift's Chamber-fellow is *said* to have seen a copy of "The Tale of a Tub," in his *own hand-writing*, Before 1688. At the

Conclusion, we learn, with astonishment, that Pope was born In the year when Swift's Chum saw the copy — consequently that he *was* born Before 1688. — Reconcile these passages who Can! — Well. — We will not stickle for a year or two. — Swift's Chum saw the copy, if not Before, at least In 1688; and Dr. Johnson *thinks* it was written between 1693 and 1697. — Here we learn, with still *greater* astonishment, that, if the Doctor be right, Swift's Chamber- fellow saw the Copy — *several years* Before It Was Written! — To crown the whole of this incomprehensible statement, we are told, in a note, ([GM] p. 1177)[274] that B.L.A. has long had *doubts* of Swift's Title to this work — that his *suspicions* are much confirmed by observing that Dr. Johnson (according to Mr. Boswell) entertained the same idea — and that B.L.A. is inclined to give the work to Mr. Anthony Henley!

Thus, Mr. Urban, we are presented — firstly, with a Report — but the Lord knows from what authority; secondly, with a Surmise the authority of Dr. Johnson, — and, thirdly, with a Suspicion the authority of B.L.A! — and, by the united force of the *report — surmise —* and *suspicion —* I am laid, it seems, sprawling on the earth! — Now let us examine the component parts of the complicated machine by which this utter "ruin" has been accomplished.

From the Report it appears probable that Swift wrote the Tale of a Tub Prior to the year 1688; from the surmise it appears probable that it was not written till some years Afterwards; and from the Suspicion it appears probable that Swift Never Wrote It At All.

I know of nothing to set in absolute *competiton* with this glorious climax of absurdity! — King Phyz's droll division in the Rehearsal approaches *near* it.

"The question is — did they hear us whisper? — Which I divide Thus; — into When they heard us whisper? — What they heard us whisper? — *and* Whether They Heard Us Whisper Or No."[275]

Joseph Weston.

---

* Till Mr Weston's promised pamphlet shall be before the publick, we think it fair to decline inserting any thing further on the subject, except the Letter of Mr. W. which is to appear in our next. Edit.

** Vol. LX. p. 1178. [Letter 28. Most of the emphasis is Weston's.]

NOTES

NOTES TO THE INTRODUCTION

1 *Physics and Beyond* (NY: Harper, 1971) 22.

2 *WA*, title page.

3 *Letters* 2:92.

4 (London: Dent, 1951) 264.

5 (London: Heinemann Educational Books, 1976) 2, 12.

6 (North Carolina: U of NC Press, 1933) 4.

7 Letter 8c. Weston quotes most of his Preface in this letter, so most references to his Preface will be to Letter 8c.

8 *Observations, Anecdotes, and Characters of Books and Men*, ed. James M. Osborn (Oxford: Clarendon, 1966) 1:24.

9 Maynard Mack discusses this in his *Life* 178-79.

10 John Dennis, *Reflections Critical and Satyrical upon a Late Rhapsody, call'd, An Essay upon Criticism*, 1711 (Yorkshire, England: Scolar Press, 1971) Preface.

11 E. N. Hooker, ed., "Letter to Jacob Tonson," *The Critical Works of John Dennis* (Baltimore: Johns Hopkins, 1939) 2:399-401. The following quotations are from that letter.

12 Letter 8c.

13 *Memoirs of the Life and Writings of Alexander Pope, Esq.* (London, 1745) 1:274, 275.

14 Shiels in Theophilus Cibber's *Lives of the Poets of Great Britain and Ireland* (London, 1753) 5:248, 249.

15 See below for Johnson's comparison.

16 *Essay* 1:iii.

17 *The Creative Imagination: Enlightenment to Romanticism* (Cambridge, Mass.: Harvard UP, 1981) 6.

18 Engell, 8..

19 "Art. V. *An Essay on the Writings and Genius of Pope*," *The Critical Review* 1:240; Dr. James Grainger's review, *The Monthly Review* 14:528-54, 15:52-78; "Review of an Essay on the Writing and Genius of Pope" from *The Literary Magazine*, 1756, in *Dr. Johnson's Works*, Oxford English Classics (Oxford, 1825) 6:37 and 46; *GM* 26:249-51, 305-06 and 52:236-40.

20 *Lives* 3:251.

21 *Rambler* 5:154.

[22] 3:223.

[23] *Lives* 1:469.

[24] M. H. Abrams traces the shift in criticism from "Pragmatic" to "Expressive," from works to writer, in *The Mirror and the Lamp* (NY: Oxford UP, 1953) 14-26.

[25] *Lives* 3:222. The quotations in the rest of the paragraph are from pages 222-23.

[26] *Letters* 1:306.

[27] *Letters* 1:187.

[28] Robert Folkenflik, *Samuel Johnson, Biographer* (Ithaca: Cornell UP, 1978) 27.

[29] Most of the letter writers signing initials or pseudonyms remain unidentified. Some are positively or tentatively identified by James Kuist in *The Nichols File of The Gentleman's Magazine* (Madison: U of Wisconsin P, 1982). I have used Kuist's identification in all cases except that of "Norfolciencis."

[30] See 1:20, 73; 2:5; 6:145, 157.

[31] For biographical information about Anna Seward I am especially indebted to Margaret Ashmun's *The Singing Swan* (NY: Greenwood Press, 1931).

[32] S. Addleshaw, "The Swan of Lichfield: Anna Seward and Her Circle," *The Church Quarterly Review* 247 (April-June, 1937):15.

[33] Quoted in Margaret Ashmun's *The Singing Swan* (NY: Greenwood P, 1931) 92.

[34] Samuel Holt Monk, "Anna Seward and the Romantic Poets," *Wordsworth and Coleridge: Studies in Honor of George McLean Harper*, ed. Leslie Griggs (Princeton: Princeton UP, 1939) 128.

[35] Ashmun, 85.

[36] Addleshaw, 22.

[37] W. C. Oulton, ed. (1813, 1822).

[38] R. W. King, *The Translator of Dante: The Life, Work and Friendships of Henry Francis Cary* (London: Martin Secker, 1925) and Grace A. Oliver, *A Study of Maria Edgeworth* (Boston, 1882).

[39] Addleshaw, 26.

[40] The correspondent "M[arcellu]s" (Henry Francis Cary), without commenting on their presence on the list of moderns, deplores their omission from the list of Pope's contemporaries (Letter 5).

[41] Ashmun, 67-68.

[42] *The Swan of Lichfield* (NY: Oxford UP, 1937) 150n.

[43] *Letters* 2:90.

[44] *Letters* 2:91-93.

[45] 58:823.

[46] "On the King's Refusal of his Sanction to the Decree against the Emigrants," 62.2:654.

47 *GM* 63.1:559-60.

48 Bloomfield's biographers describe Weston as the man "who knew him so well." William Wickett and Nicholas Duval, *The Farmer's Boy* (Lavenham, England: Terence Dalton, 1971) 62.

49 "Preface" to *The Remains of Robert Bloomfield* x.

50 King, *The Translator of Dante* 7.

51 King, 22.

52 Cary's biographer can find no clear reason why he adopted this particular name. See King, 18-19.

53 Quoted in C. Lennart Carlson, *The First Magazine: A History of The Gentleman's Magazine* (Providence: Brown U, 1938) 29-30. For information about the *GM*, I am indebted to this book and to John Nichols's "The Rise and Progress of *The Gentleman's Magazine*," *General Index* to the *GM* (1821) 3:iii-lxxx.

54 Arthur Sherbo, "Additions to the Nichols File of the *Gentleman's Magazine*," *Studies in Bibliography* (1984) 37:229.

55 In "The Rise and Progress of *The Gentleman's Magazine*," Nichols calls Johnson "my illustrious Predecessor," 3:iii.

56 Carlson, 27.

57 Carlson, 28.

58 Carlson, 197.

59 Carlson, 196.

60 *GM* 59.2:780.

61 *Twk* 5:439.

62 Weston quotes Pope's note in Letter 14.

63 Warton's comparison of Pope's and Dryden's styles is discussed above.

64 Miss Seward's quotation has "Shall." Even in quoting Dryden, she unconsciously revises his diction.

NOTES TO THE LETTERS

1 (Birmingham, 1788). For biographical information about John Morfitt and Joseph Weston see "The Controversialists" section of the Introduction.

2 Letter 8c. Miss Seward paraphrases Weston's words, which were that he had traced "the insidious Arts which he [Pope] suffered his *Friends* to practise, in order to undermine the Reputation of the deceased Poet and to asperse the Characters of his living Supporters."

3 Unidentified.

4 Letter 8c.

5 See Appendix, Part 1.

6 London, 1751.

[7] London and Dublin, 1724.

[8] Published in *The Repository*, ed. Isaac Reed (London, 1777-1783).

[9] Letter 8c.

[10] Letter 8c.

[11] Anna Seward says substantially the same thing in a letter to John Morfitt, dated Feb. 7, 1789. *Letters* 2:239-40.

[12] Letter 8c.

[13] Matthew Prior and Charles Montagu, *The Hind and the Panther Transvers'd to the Story of The Country Mouse and the City-Mouse* in *The Literary Works of Matthew Prior*, ed. H. Bunker Wright and Monroe K. Spears (Oxford: Clarendon, 1959) 1:40.

[14] Prior *Works*, 1:35-6. Miss Seward has remembered the sense and much of the wording accurately. She conflates two passages from the original and changes a few words. Her greatest deviation from the original occurs in the two sentences beginning "How can we conceive a panther reading" and ending "ranging in forests." Instead, read "What relation has the Hind to our Saviour? or what notion have we of a Panther's Bible? If you say he means the Church, how does the Church feed on lawns, or range in the Forest?"

[15] *WA* xix.

[16] Letter 8c.

[17] Unidentified.

[18] Letter 8c.

[19] Read "like naves, our Venus soil?"

[20] Read "She for the Fault of one offending Foe".

[21] Shakespeare, *The Merry Wives of Windsor* III.v.124. For "Master Ford" read "Master Brooke."

[22] Probably a conflation of various eighteenth-century authors. David Erskine and Isaac Reed wrote that Dryden was driven to "writing for mere bread," *Biographica Dramatica* (London, 1812) 1:202. Pope's biographer, Owen Ruffhead, reported that Pope used to say of Dryden's poetry that he "would have been perfect in it had he not been so often obliged to write with precipitation," *The Life of Alexander Pope, Esq.* (London, 1769) 23. William Ayre noted the same thing in *Memoirs* 1:247.

[23] Milton, *A Mask* (Comus) 349.

[24] Letter 8c and *WA* xx.

[25] *Lives* 1:469.

[26] Unidentified.

[27] Read "And with paternal thunder vindicates her crown." Johnson had remembered the line incorrectly. See *Lives* 1:469n.

[28] *WA* xxi-xxii.

[29] *WA* xxii-xxiii.

30   The ballad "Captain Chilver's Gone to Sea" closely resembles this, except for the prosaic fifth line, which Miss Seward may have invented to reinforce her point. See *The Roxburghe Ballads*, ed. J. Woodfall Ebsworth, (Hertford: Ballad Society, 1890) 7.1:529.

31   Letter 8c.

32   Letter 8c.

33   See *Ep2* 24, "As Sappho's diamonds with her dirty smock."

34   In this letter to the *GM* of November 6, 1788, Weston wrote in a P.S.:

> Before I entirely conclude this long appeal, I must, in the name of every friend to worth and ingenuity, justice and humanity, thank your indefatigable Editor, for having so generously and spiritedly rescued the writings of a worthy and most elegant poet, from that oblivion to which they were hastening, through the vile arts of a jealous tyrant, not less remarkable for meanness than for malignity, equally distinguished by cowardice and by cruelty! It is almost unnecessary to add, that, by the former, I mean the excellent *Welsted*; and, by the latter, the execrable *Pope*!

35   Pope had satirized Leonard Welsted in *Dunciad*(A), comparing him to his "inspirer, Beer,/ Tho' stale, not ripe; tho' thin, yet never clear;" (5:3.163-64). Welsted and and fellow dunce, James Moore Smythe, retaliated in *One Epistle to Mr. Pope* (1730).

36   *Aeneid*, 2:521-22. For "Seward" read "tempus." "Not such the aid nor these the defences the hour craves."

37   William Hayley, *Essay on Epic Poetry, Poems and Plays* (Dublin, 1788) 3:4.91. Read "lovely Train."

38   Letter 1a.

39   Letter 8c.

40   See Letter 18.

41   Weston complains because Johnson did not include Davenant in his *Lives*.

42   Johnson noted that Villiers' play, *The Rehearsal*, initially had Davenant as its satirical target, *Lives* 1:369. Villiers was also credited with an anonymous poem ridiculing Davenant's *Gondibert*, "Verses on the Preface of *Gondibert*." This is no longer believed to be by Villiers. See *Buckingham: Public and Private Man.*, ed. Christine Phipps (NY: Garland, 1985) 260.

43   See Appendix, Part 3. Johnson wrote *Lives* of all these men.

44   Probably a paraphrase of Luke 1.52: "He hath put down the mighty from their seats, and exalted them of low degree."

45   William Davenant, Stanza 10, "The Christian's Reply to the Phylosopher," *Poems on Several Occasions, Works* (London, 1673) 334-35.

46   See Appendix, Part 4.

47   Letter 4.

48   Letter 4.

49 These are not Weston's words. "M.F." may have ascribed them to Weston by accident.

50 Letter 5.

51 Most of William Shenstone's works were published before 1744. James Hammond, who is not on Miss Seward's third list, published his elegies during the 1730s. William Somervile's poems gained in popularity after his death in 1742. At least half of David Mallet's works were published before 1744, including his collected Works in 1743. Also see Appendix, Part 1.

52 George Villiers. See Appendix, Parts 1 amd 4.

53 Miss Seward added Lyttleton, Ansty, Mickle, and Jekyll to her third list in Letter 1b. See Appendix, Part 2. Richard Polwhele and Thomas Tickell are listed in the *NCBEL* and the *DNB*.

54 The *DNB* describes John Pomfret as poet and John Dennis as a critic, poet, and playwright. They are both listed in *NCBEL*.

55 James Thomson's major work, *The Seasons*, was published in individual parts between 1726 and 1728, and as a whole in 1730. It had run to many editions before his death in 1748.

56 Letter 1b. Miss Seward's references are to that letter unless otherwise noted.

57 Letter 5.

58 Letter 6.

59 "Speak no ill of the dead," Plutarch, *Lives* (Solon), Sec. 21.

60 Letter 6.

61 "Let justice be done, though the heavens fall," proverbial.

62 In this letter, all the quotations from "M.F." are from Letter 6.

63 This poem does not appear in Weston's published works. I have been unable to find any record of his unpublished papers.

64 *Dramatic Poesy*, 2:84. Dryden wrote of Milton, "his thoughts are elevated, his words sounding.... 'Tis true, he runs into a flat of thought, sometimes for a hundred lines together."

65 "M — — s" says in Letter 5. "That Dryden purposely kept down certain parts of his writings, in order to serve as foils to the rest, is an assertion in which Mr. W. will not, perhaps, find a single advocate; as the prematurity in which pecuniary circumstances compelled him to hurry his publications into the world is known and lamented by every one."

66 "The evening of a royal birthday... the court-festival held thereon," *OED*.

67 *Lives* 3: 222.

68 John Dennis, *A True Character of Mr. Pope, Works*, ed. E. N. Hooker, 2:108.

69 Weston seems to be freely paraphrasing what Joseph Spence recorded that Pope said of Walsh, "He encouraged me much, and used to tell me, that there was one way left of excelling: for though we had several great poets, we never had any one great poet that was correct; and he desired me to make that my study and aim," Spence, 32.

70 *Arbu* 4:136.

71 Horace, *The Art of Poetry* 5, "Could you refrain from laughing?"

72 Horace advised, "put your parchment in the closet and keep it back till the ninth year," *The Art of Poetry*, 388-89.

73 See Letter 6.

74 I have been unable to identify the source of this in William Hayley's works. In his "Essay on Epic Poetry," Hayley wrote: "Milton's Verse, and Dryden's Rhyme,/ Are proof alike against the rage of Time," *Poems and Plays* (1788), 3: 5.233-34.

75 *WA* vii-xv.

76 "A Grammar of the English Tongue," *Dictionary* (1755). Read, "The pause in the Alexandrine must be at the sixth syllable."

77 *WA* xxiii-xxiv.

78 Letter 1a.

79 Letter 1b.

80 See above, toward the end of Weston's quotation from his "Preface." The following quotations are from the same place.

81 Letter 1b.

82 "Prologue, Spoken at the Opening of the Theatre in Drury-Lane, 1747," *Works* 6:3.

83 William Hayley, "Revolution Ode." This line and the one before it are quoted in the *GM* 59:27. I have been unable to find the entire poem.

84 Thomas Gray, "The Progress of Poesy," 35. Samuel Johnson noted, "Gray is too fond of words arbitrarily compounded. 'Many-twinkling' was formerly censured as not analogical; we may say *many-spotted*, but scarcely *many-spotting*" (*Lives*, 3:437).

85 Letter 1b. The quotations in this and the next paragraph are from the same place.

86 Letter 1b.

87 *WA* xviii.

88 Letter 1b.

89 Pope, *Il* 8:10.511.

90 Shakespeare, *King John*, IV.ii. 11-12. Read "to gild refined gold, to paint the lily, to throw a perfume on the violet."

91 *Epl* 3.2:6.

92 Virgil, *Aeneid* 6.276, "ill-prompting hunger." Dryden rendered it "Famine's unresisted rage" (*Ae* 3:6.387).

93 Written source unidentified.

94 Unidentified.

95 Weston corrects this "evident Blunder" in Letter 24.

96 Unidentified.

[97] Shakespeare, *The Tempest* IV.i.152.

[98] *Longinus on the Sublime*, trans. William Smith (Baltimore, 1810) 23-27.

[99] Letter 1b.

[100] Letter to John Morfitt dated February 7, 1789 (*Letters* 2:237). Miss Seward's actual words were "the magic curve, so dear to beauty."

[101] Henry Home, Lord Kames, *Elements of Criticism* (Edinburgh, 1762) 2:88. "No man contracts a habit of taking sugar, honey, or sweet-meats, as he doth of tobacco."

[102] Probably a paraphrase of "upon faint primrose beds were wont to lie," Shakespeare, *A Midsummer-Night's Dream* I.i.215.

[103] Virgil, *Aeneid* 6.545, "I will go my way; I will fill up the tale and get me back to the darkness."

[104] Letter 1b.

[105] Letter 1b.

[106] Letter 1b.

[107] *Lives* 3:229.

[108] Andrews, Fellow of the Antiquarian Society, wrote, "The great Jonathan Swift, Dean of St. Patrick's made his 'debut' in the literary world, by one of the wretchedest odes which ever disgraced Grub-street" (1790).

[109] Letter 1b.

[110] Letter 7.

[111] "But *Sense* surviv'd, when *merry Jests* were past," *EOC* 460.

[112] In 1679, Dryden collaborated with John Sheffield (Earl of Mulgrave and Marquis of Normanby, later Duke of Buckingham) on a translation of Ovid's epistle, *Helen to Paris*.

[113] For excerpts from *Helen to Paris*, see Letter 1b.

[114] "Comparable to the cruel action of Mezentius, a mythical Etruscan king, who caused living men to be bound face to face with corpses, and left to die of starvation, Virgil, *Aeneid* 8.485-88," *OED*.

[115] Matthew Prior, "A Satyr on the Modern Translators," 39-40.

[116] The *Essay upon Satire*, which contained an unflattering portrait of John Wilmot, second Earl of Rochester, circulated in manuscript in November 1679. When Dryden was assaulted in Rose Alley a few weeks later, people asssumed that Rochester had hired the assailants. Dryden's biographer has concluded that Rochester was not involved. See Charles Ward, *The Life of John Dryden* (Chapel Hill: U of North Carolina P, 1961) 353n.

[117] Unidentified. In 1681, Mulgrave admitted he was the author of the *Essay* (Ward, 144).

[118] "Either Erasmus or the Devil," proverbial.

[119] *Essay upon Poetry* published anonymously (Dublin, 1682).

[120] Pope's note to this line ascribes it to the Duke of Buckingham's *Essay on Poetry* (1717).

121 "At my risk," a commonplace found in Plautus and Cicero.

122 Weston seems to be mistaken. I can find no record of this among John Sheffield's (Mulgrave's) works. The *BM* Catalogue does not list it.

123 Ovid, *Heroides* 7.177-96.

124 *Ep3* 262-90.

125 Warton 2:170-71.

126 Letter 1c. Mack notes that according to a letter from Pope to David Mallet in 1733 "Pope had, it seems clear, been contributing financial aid to Dennis surreptitiously through Mallet," *Life* 588.

127 *Prologue, for the Benefit of Mr. Dennis, 1733* at a performance of Colley Cibber's *The Provok'd Husband*, Dec. 18, 1733, *Twk* 6:355.57.

128 *Original Letters, Familiar, Moral and Critical*, 2 vols. (1721).

129 Probably the 1735 edition.

130 George Sherburne, ed., *Correspondence of Alexander Pope* (Oxford: Clarendon, 1956) 2:75-76. The letter was originally published by John Dennis in his *Remarks Upon the Dunciad* (Hooker 2:370-71).

131 Letter 1c.

132 Letter 8c.

133 *HE* 4:2.1.08.

134 *Lives* 3:126-27. Johnson recounts how Halifax told Pope to revise passages in the first three books of his *Iliad* to give them "a little [better] turn." Dismayed, Pope asked Garth's advice, and Garth recommended that Pope leave the passages untouched and reread them to Halifax in a few months as if he had changed them. Pope did so, and Halifax "was extremely pleased with them, and cried out, 'Ay, now [Mr. Pope] they are perfectly right: nothing can be better.'"

135 Letter 1c.

136 Letter 1c.

137 Weston may be partially remembering Horace's words, "Take from the verses which I am writing now ... their regular beat and rhythm — change the order of the words, transposing the first and the last — and it would not be like breaking up ... where, even when he is dismembered, you would find the limbs of a poet" (*Satires* 1.4.56-62).

138 Letter 9. Anna Seward's references to Morfitt are to this letter.

139 Letter 7.

140 Letter 1c, note 23.

141 Milton, *Paradise Lost* 4.631.

142 *Merchant of Venice* V.i.54. Read "this bank."

143 *Romeo and Juliet* II.ii.108.

144 *2 Henry VI* IV.i.3.

145 Letter 8d.

[146] Letter 7. "M — —s's" references are to this letter, except where noted.

[147] Pope praised *Pleasures of the Imagination* when it appeared in 1744. Maynard Mack cites Johnson's *Lives* (Akenside) 3:412 (*Life* 924).

[148] 1743 and 1742 respectively.

[149] For Hammond and Mallet see note 51; for Thomson and Lyttleton notes 55 and 53 respectively. George Lyttleton's works began appearing in 1728, but no collection was published until the year after his death in 1773.

[150] Leonard Welsted is not on Miss Seward's lists. He is listed in *NCBEL* and *DNB*.

[151] Sir Samuel Garth (c. 1660-1718). "M — —s" refers to Miss Seward's three lists of poets in Letter 1a.

[152] George Granville, Baron Lansdowne; William Walsh, Pope's early mentor; William Wycherley; and Sir William Trumbull (died c. 1716-17), Pope's neighbor and "second father," see Mack, *Life of Pope* (104-09). All these, together with Elijah Fenton and William Broome, are listed in the *DNB* and all, except for Trumbull, are listed in the *NCBEL*.

[153] Letter 1a. Miss Seward lists only one "Philips."

[154] *Letters of Thomas Gray*, ed. Duncan C. Tovey (London: G. Bell and Sons, 1912) 3:95. Gray made the remark in a letter to Thomas Wharton. He was repeating what he had said to James Beattie in conversation.

[155] Thomas Warton (London, 1870) 243.

[156] Exact source unidentified. This may be "M.F.'s" reference to what had become a commonplace about Pope. See Ayre, *Memoirs* 1:242. Even Colley Cibber wrote that Pope appeared "to have had personal provocation" for his satire in *The Dunciad*. See *An Apology for the Life of Colley Cibber*, ed. B. R. S. Stone (Ann Arbor: The U of Michigan P, 1968, 26).

[157] Livy, Book 34, Ch. 28, sec. 3.

[158] Religious reformer John Wycliffe was buried in 1384. In 1428, by order of the Council of Constance, his body was disinterred, burnt and thrown into a nearby river (*DNB*).

[159] This classical scholar and author of religious works may be the "gloomy clerk" referred to in *DunB* 5:4.459ff. and note.

[160] For John Hughes (or possibly Jabez Hughes) and Aaron Hill see the appendix to *DunA* 5:2.283n.; for John Hervey, first Baron of Ickworth, see *HS* 4:2.1.6; for James Brydges, Duke of Chandos see *Ep4* 3.2:99n.

[161] Weston quotes an edition of *Dunciad* A, other than the first, in which letters were used instead of names. For Pope's treatment of Thomas Burnet and George Duckett see the "The Issues" section of the Introduction. The "REMARKS" are Pope's note to line 175 and include the epigram.

[162] Published as *The Hump Conference* in 1715, changed to *Homerides* in 1716.

[163] "A serpent supposed to have two heads." Johnson, *Dictionary*.

[164] *Works* 2nd ed. (London, 1728). Read "You are known to have that Respect, Esteem, and Affection for the most beautiful Part of the Creation which

God and Nature design'd we should have... These Qualities which have recommended You to a very fine Lady, to whom You have been married many Years, and by Whom You had Eight Children."

165 Hooker 2:314. Pope condensed Dennis's remarks.

166 Duckett died in 1732; Burnet was appointed a judge for the court of common pleas in 1741.

167 Letter 8c. Miss Seward conflates Weston's words.

168 *Palaemon to Celia at Bath, or the Triumvirate* (1717). See *Dun*A 5:2.293n.

169 Letter 14.

170 Letter 8d. Weston quoted lines 56-75 from Dryden's *Aeneid* Miss Seward misquotes the beginnings of lines 60 and 62.

171 Miss Seward quotes from *The Hind and the Panther* (Letter 10) and from Dryden's Virgil (Letter 1b). She does not quote from the *Ode on the Death of Anne Killigrew*, but she does quote *Upon the Death of the Lord Hastings* (Letter 1b).

172 Letter 8d.

173 Letter 8d.

174 Erasmus Darwin (Lichfield and London, 1789) 2.425.26. For Anna Seward's relations with Darwin see "The Controversialists" section of the Introduction.

175 William Hayley, "Ode Inscribed to John Howard," *Poems and Plays* (1788) 1:131.

176 Weston simply called Pope "execrable," Letter 2. "M. F." lengthened the epithet to "execrable impostor," Letter 12.

177 Letter 8b.

178 Quoted in Ruffhead, *Life* 500.

179 Joseph Addison, *Spectator* 378.

180 Letter 8b. Read "M.F. exultingly asks."

181 Possibly a partial quotation of the speech by Acres, "my valour is certainly going! — it is sneaking off! — I feel it oozing out as it were at the palms of my hands!" (Richard Sheridan, *The Rivals* V.iii. 93-95).

182 Letter 9. All "M.F.'s" references to Morfitt are to this letter.

183 Unidentified.

184 1:24-25.

185 Letter 14.

186 Letter 14.

187 Letter 15.

188 Johnson discusses Pope's character in *Lives* 3:196-215. For a critique of Johnson see Maynard Mack, "Reflections of an Amateur Biographer," *Modern Language Review* (October 1984) 79.4:xxix-xxx.

189 *A Tale of a Tub* with *The Battle of the Books*, A.C. Gulthkelch and D. Nichol Smith, eds. (Oxford: Clarendon, 1958) 247.

[190] Gulthkelch and Smith, 36.

[191] Weston discusses the Burnet and Duckett issue in Letter 14. Also, see "The Issues" section of the Introduction.

[192] Letter 14.

[193] Poem "To Miss Seward," *GM* 60.1:162.

[194] Weston actually wrote, "As this is the last Notice which I intend to take of an *anonymous* Correspondent," Letter 14.

[195] Letter 21.

[196] "He that is without sin among you, let him first cast a stone at her," John 8.7. Guilt.

[197] Letter 10.

[198] In *Homerides*, see Letter 14.

[199] Unidentified.

[200] See Letter 14 and note 161.

[201] Letter 18.

[202] Letters 7 and 10.

[203] Letter 1b.

[204] Letter 1b.

[205] Letter 8d.

[206] Letter 15, Weston's emphasis.

[207] Possibly a partial quotation of Millamant's exclamation, "odious men! I hate your odious provisos," William Congreve, *The Way of the World* (1700) IV.i.247.

[208] John 11:35 in Edward Harwood, *A Liberal Translation of the New Testament* (London, 1768), 1:328.

[209] Letter 15. The quotations in this and the next paragraph are from this letter, except where noted.

[210] 1.36-37.

[211] 1.4. "Through cruel Juno's unforgiving wrath."

[212] Letter 1b.

[213] Letter 15. Weston adds some of the emphases.

[214] Letter 8d.

[215] The *British Museum Cataloque* lists editions for 1683, 1701, 1705, 1712, 1720, and 1725.

[216] Letter 8d.

[217] Letter 9.

[218] Letter 15.

[219] Letter 8d.

[220] Letter 8c.

221 Letter 8d.

222 Letter 10.

223 Letter 15.

224 *Heroides* 7:13-26.

225 Unidentified. This translation is not listed under Mulgrave in the *British Museum Catalogue*. To my knowledge, it does not appear among his published works.

226 Letter 10.

227 See Weston's discussion in Letters 14 and 20. Also see "The Issues" section of the Introduction.

228 "Nisus and Euryalus foremost — Euryalus famed for beauty and flower of youth, Nisus for tender love for the boy," 5.294-96.

229 "Nisus was guardian of the gate.... At his side was Euryalus.... A common love was theirs; side by side they charge in the fray; now too they together were mounting sentry at the gate," 9.176, 179, 182-83.

230 Settle (1648-1724) was a playwright and poet, as was Colley Cibber (1671-1757). Charles Gildon (1665-1724) was a poet, playwright and critic. They are all listed in the *DNB* and *NCBEL*.

231 Letter 14.

232 *Satire* ii.1.86.

233 Letter 14.

234 Letter 19.

235 Joseph Spence, *An Essay on Mr. Pope's Odyssey* (London, 1737) 246-47.

236 "And willing Nations knew their Lawfull Lord."

237 Weston apparently forgot that the opening paragraph of his quotation from Spence mentions "some Thoughts wove into this Translation... from Dryden."

238 Letter 9.

239 *One Epistle to Mr. A. Pope (1730)* 20.

240 Shakespeare, *King Lear*, IV.vi.107.

241 Weston first uses the term "Adversary" for "M. F." in Letter 4. This quotation seems to be an extension of his own.

242 Letter 18.

243 Read "Accipe nunc Danaum." "Hear now the treachery of the Greeks and from one learn the wickedness of all" (Virgil, *Aeneid* 2.65).

244 Letter 9.

245 Letter 10.

246 "Never was a creature so inconsistent" (Horace, *Satires* I.iii.18).

247 From *Ordovices*, the "name of an ancient British tribe in North Wales" (*OED*).

248 Jonathan Swift, "A Libel on the Reverend Dr. Delaney and His Excellency John Lord Carteret," *The Complete Poems of Johnathan Swift*, ed. Pat Rogers (Harmondsworth, Eng.: Penguin, 1983) 80.

249 Read "Uti nunc possidetis," "Thus, as you now possess." Sextus Pompeius Festus, *De Verborum Significatu Quae Supersunt Cum Paul Epitome*, ed. Wallace M. Lindsay (Hildesheim, Ger.: Georg Olms, 1965) 260.

250 See Letter 14.

251 David Dalrymple is mistaken. The original title, *The Hump Conference*, clearly points to Pope. See Mack, *Life* 277.

252 Letter 1a.

253 Letter 18.

254 Pope, "Preface" to Homer's *Iliad* 5:22.

255 Letter 21.

256 Shakespeare, *Richard III*. V.v. The fight occurs at the beginning of the scene.

257 Letter 32. All quotations from Weston are from this letter.

258 Letter 28, note (3).

259 Anthony Ashley Cooper, Earl of Shaftesbury, *Characteristics of Men, Manners, Opinions, Times*, ed. John M. Robertson (NY: Bobbs-Merrill) 2:328-29, 333.

260 Letter 15.

261 "From furious *Sappho* scarce a milder Fate,/P — x'd by her Love, or libell'd by her Hate" (*First Satire of the Second Book of Horace. Imitated* 4:83-84). Sappho is Lady Mary Wortley Montagu.

262 See William Ayre, *MemoirS*. Discussing Pope's imitation of the *First Satire of the Second Book of Horace*, Ayre wrote that it was said to be aimed at a "Lady of Quality," (Lady Mary Wortley Montagu), but he does not cite the lines because they are "too harsh" (2:197).

263 *Od* 9:11.776.

264 Letter 32.

265 Letter 33.

266 Shakespeare, *Othello* II.1.161.

267 Letter 34.

268 Weston wrote no further letters to the *GM*.

269 Weston did not publish this pamphlet.

270 Letter 33. The following references are to that letter unless otherwise noted.

271 Letter 32. Weston chastised "B. L. A." for misreading his letter (18) in which he explained that he had not said Pope incited or instigated his friends to undermine Dryden's reputation, but merely "suffered" them to do so.

272 Johnson defined classical as "relating to antique authors; relating to literature." He defined critical as "exact; nicely judicious; accurate; diligent."

273 Samuel Foote (London, 1776) III.ii.119-20, p. 69. The speaker is Margin.

274 Letter 28, note (3).

275 George Villiers, Duke of Buckingham, II.iv.8-9, 15-16. Weston conflates two speeches by the Gentleman-Usher.

APPENDIX

1. Regarding Anna Seward's three lists of poets, I assume that Milton, Dryden, Pope, Prior, Gay, Swift, Addison, Congreve, Steele, Gray, Thomson, Cowper, Goldsmith, Johnson, Sheridan, Walpole, Crabbe, Garrick, Burns, and Chatterton need no further identification. Of the remainder, all but four can be found in the *DNB*, and most can also be found in the *NCBEL*. Those names with asterisks can be found only in the *DNB*. For the four names not found in either source, I have supplied dates and brief identifications.

First List: Thomas Otway, Abraham Cowley, Edmund Waller, Sir William Davenant, Samuel Butler, John Denham, Nathaniel Lee, Wentworth Dillon (Earl of Roscommon).

Second List: Edward Young, Thomas Tickell, Nicholas Rowe, Thomas Parnell, Dr. John Arbuthnot, either Ambrose Philips or John Philips (M — —s assumes it is not Ambrose because he reproves Miss Seward for omitting "A. Philips" from her list (Letter 5)), Isaac Watts, Lady Mary Wortley Montagu.

Third List: William Hayley, William Mason, William Collins, Mark Akenside, Joseph Warton and Thomas Warton the younger, Robert Jephson, James Beattie, Charles Churchill, William Shenstone, John Langhorne, Sir William Jones, Henry James Pye, David Mallet, Richard Owen Cambridge, Bishop Robert Lowth or Louth. John Sargent (not Sarjent), died in 1831. (*GM* 1831, ii:285 amd *Biog. Dram.* 1812, 3:43) He wrote *The Mine*, a dramatic poem, which William Hayley commented on in his *Memoirs* as rivalling Milton's *Comus*. Anna Seward mentions Sargent's other two poems, both odes, in her *Letters* 2:259. Thomas Whalley, Thomas James Mathias, Edward Jerningham, William Whitehead, Charles James Fox*, Robert Lloyd*, Samuel Wesley the younger, John Dyer, John Hoole. Rev. Samuel Hoole (c. 1758-1839), John Hoole's brother, published a volume of poems which included *The Curate* (1788), a volume of *Sermons* (1790), and *Anecdotes* (1804) of his brother John. He also translated *The Selected Works of A. van Leeuwenhoek, containing his Microscopical Discoveries* (1798). Isaac Hawkins Browne, William Somervile (or Somerville), probably minor playwright John Home rather than Scottish judge and scholar Henry Home

(Lord Kames), William Crowe, George Steevens (not Stevens), Arthur Murphy. De la Crusca (or Della Crusca) is the pseudonym of Robert Merry, who adopted it from the famous Florentine Academy. Richard Cumberland, Bertie Greathead*, Theophilus Swift*, either Edward Barry* or George Barry*, George Butt.* Peter Pindar was the pseudonym of John Wolcot. John Cunningham and Thomas Mounsey Cunningham*, Anna Barbauld, Hannah More, Anna Williams, Hester Thrale Piozzi, Elizabeth Carter, Hannah Cowley, Charlotte (not Catherine) Smith, Henry Francis Cary.* Thomas Lister (1772-1828) lived in Lichfield and, along with Cary, contributed poetry to the *GM*. At the time of this controversy, Lister and Cary were schoolboy protegés of Anna Seward. John Newton, Mrs. Ann Yearsley, and William Reid.*

2. George Lyttelton, Christopher Anstey, William Julius Mickle, and Joseph Jekyll are listed in the *DNB* and all but Jekyll are listed in the *NCBEL*.

3. Richard Duke, George Stepney, Thomas Yalden, and John Pomfret are listed in the *DNB* and *NCBEL*.

4. Miss Seward puts Akenside, Collins, Thomson, Mallet, Shenstone, and Somervile on her third list of poets in the period succeeding Pope's. She defends this division in her Letter 7. She adds George Lyttleton to the third list in her Letter 1b. She mentions Allan Ramsay in her third list when she says Burns is his successor. She mentions Philips in her third list, but "M — —s" assumes she means John Philips. She makes no mention of James Hammond, Leonard Welsted, Richard Glover, William Broome, John Pomfret, neither Jabez Hughes nor John Hughes, Sir Samuel Garth, George Villiers (Duke of Buckingham), nor John Dennis. They are all listed in the *DNB* and the *NCBEL*.

Manufactured by Amazon.ca
Bolton, ON

26283903R00087